Praise for *The Power of Purpose*

'I have long believed that clarity of purpose is a key enabler in the delivery of sustainable long-term value for all stakeholders. John and Andrew's book shows how to find, spread and follow such purpose within organisations and is a meaningful contribution to this debate.'

Paul Polman, Chief Executive, Unilever

'A rising generation of leaders are increasingly concerned about the social purpose of any business they might work for. This book will be invaluable for companies wanting to build and communicate a genuine sense of purpose, aligned with their values and vision, as a means of attracting and retaining the best talent.'

Dame Polly Courtice DBE, LVO, Director,
The Cambridge Programme for Sustainable Leadership

'*The Power of Purpose* provides an essential insight as to how building a business with a true and genuine sense of purpose can transform your company and your culture.'

Lord Verjee CBE, Chairman, Thomas Goode & Co;
Founder, Domino's Pizza

'Manifest success in raising living standards in our free market/capitalist economic system has seldom been so much criticised and called into doubt. . . . *The Power of Purpose* will help people understand the good that business can do in the world and so at the same time give all who lead or work in business a renewed sense of the meaning and purpose in what they do.'

Lord Lamont PC,
former Chancellor of the Exchequer

'*The Power of Purpose* is an essential part of any business leader's reading and the best possible guide on how to stay on track, keep focused and achieve results. It addresses the "Why?" which sits at the centre of any mission and the purpose behind reaching the "How".'

Roddy Gow OBE, Chairman and Founder,
The Asia Scotland Institute

'*The Power of Purpose* provides compelling insights into what really matters. A must read, it is essentially a manifesto for success.'

Pinky Lilani CBE, DL, Founder, 'Spice Magic',
'Women of the Future', 'Asian Women of Achievement'

'This book offers a rare and remarkable blend of experience, insight and practical advice in how to build a greater purpose in business and life. It is an essential ingredient to anyone's future success.'

Professor Binna Kandola OBE,
Chairman, PearnKandola

'The UN's 2030 Agenda for Sustainable Development consists of 17 Sustainable Development Goals that serve as a blueprint for creating a better humanity. These goals cannot be achieved by one government or organisation alone; they require the active engagement of individuals, social entrepreneurs, companies and foundations alike. This book eloquently lays out excellent ideas for people to get behind a mission in life that can bring about positive social change in society. The days of traditional CSR are over, and we need to engage the business community and encourage companies to alter their DNA so that their core business model serves as a basis for doing well and doing good. By highlighting the mission of global business leaders, I have no doubt that you will inspire many others to emulate social good initiatives.'

Amir A. Dossal, President, Global Partnerships Forum;
former Chief Liaison Officer for Partnerships, United Nations

'I am so pleased John and Andrew have shared their extensive experience on organisational purpose. As entrepreneurs, many of us found purpose much later in life and if I had to do it all over again, this is an aspect I would pay credence to sooner rather than later. Therein lies a message for all budding entrepreneurs, to consider the Six Steps of finding *your* business purpose.'

Shabir Randeree CBE, Chancellor, East London University;
Chairman, DCD London & Mutual PLC

'*The Power of* Purpose arrived at a perfect time for me. As a female founder of a rapidly growing digital health company, I wanted to make sure that patient value and impact was at the DNA of everything we do. How to ensure that was more of a challenge. Reading this really helped me articulate my thoughts into action.'

Dr Elin Haf Davies PhD, Atlantic rower;
CEO and Founder, Aparito

'*The Power of Purpose* is an extraordinary balance of thought-provoking insights and constructive action plans for unlocking personal, professional and corporate potential. Leaders who understand the power of "doing well by doing good" simply must read this book.'

Julie Lyle, Chair Emerita,
Global Retail Marketing Association

'If we need to learn a lesson from the 2008 financial crash and recent corporate failures, it's that we must put purpose and social innovation back at the core of doing business. In this book, John and Andrew build on the examples of senior business leaders – and their experiences – and show you how.'

Dominic Llewellyn, CEO, Numbers for Good

'*The Power of Purpose* makes clear the case for meaningful purpose in any business and the benefits of staying true to this at every stage. Whether you're setting up a new venture or leading a blue-chip giant, this is a must-read for today's business leader.'

Sophie Cornish MBE, Co-Founder, Notonthehighstreet.com

'*The Power of Purpose* should be required reading for everyone who is *really* interested in business. It is a detailed and fascinating exposition of that most fundamental pillar of all successful and enduring businesses: clarity of purpose.'

Des Gunewardena, Chairman and Chief Executive, D&D
Restaurants (formerly Conran Restaurants)

'Purposeful business is an idea whose time has come. A mission to do good while doing well can transform both business and society, as long as it pursued seriously rather than as cosmetic "social washing". John O' Brien and Andrew Cave explain how the best companies are getting it right.'

Matthew Bishop, Senior Sditor, The Economist Group; author,
Philanthrocapitalism

'In today's world of work, Millennials of Generation Y are becoming a greater proportion of our workforce. It is clear that the motivators for this generation are different from the past. They are more motivated by a sense of purpose and working for an organisation that has a higher moral code. As leaders in business we must understand our workforce and be able to provide an environment where all are able to meet their own personal needs for fulfilment. This is where this excellent book provides guidance and understanding on how to create a sense of purpose and unite the workforce through setting altruistic but business focused goals. In my experience, the principles and teachings of this book will help to engage the workforce, which will result in improved staff satisfaction, greater staff retention and ultimately enhanced productivity. This book is a roadmap for improving your ethically driven performance.'

Richard Huw Lewis MBE, Managing Director, MPCT

'John and Andrew's work on *The Power of Purpose* is a must read to understand how world-class performing organisations and individuals fully understand their clarity of purpose and unlock their potential to not only deliver financial profits but also create a positive societal impact and lasting legacy.'

Jason Gardener MBE, President, UK Athletics;
Olympic 100m relay gold medallist

'An inspiring work from important authors. In a time of frivolity, *The Power of Purpose* is a game-changer and as one of those truly outstanding reads, critical to achieving your success!'

Alysia Silberg, UN Women,
Empower Women Global Champion

The Power of Purpose

Pearson

At Pearson, we have a simple mission: to help people make more of their lives through learning.

We combine innovative learning technology with trusted content and educational expertise to provide engaging and effective learning experiences that serve people wherever and whenever they are learning.

From classroom to boardroom, our curriculum materials, digital learning tools and testing programmes help to educate millions of people worldwide – more than any other private enterprise.

Every day our work helps learning flourish and, wherever learning flourishes, so do people.

To learn more, please visit us at **www.pearson.com/uk**

The Power of Purpose

Inspire teams, engage customers, transform business

John O'Brien and Andrew Cave

 Pearson

Harlow, England • London • New York • Boston • San Francisco • Toronto • Sydney
Dubai • Singapore • Hong Kong • Tokyo • Seoul • Taipei • New Delhi
Cape Town • São Paulo • Mexico City • Madrid • Amsterdam • Munich • Paris • Milan

PEARSON EDUCATION LIMITED
Edinburgh Gate
Harlow CM20 2JE
United Kingdom
Tel: +44 (0)1279 623623
Web: www.pearson.com/uk

First edition published 2017 (print and electronic)

ISBN: 978-1-292-20204-4 (print)
      978-1-292-20061-3 (PDF)
      978-1-292-20060-6 (ePub)

British Library Cataloguing-in-Publication Data
A catalogue record for the print edition is available from the British Library

Library of Congress Cataloging-in-Publication Data
A catalog record for the print edition is available from the Library of Congress

10 9 8 7 6 5 4 3
21 20 19 18

Cover design by redeyoffdesign.com
Images on front cover and chapter title pages © littleWhale/Shutterstock.com and VLADGRIN/Shutterstock.com
Print edition typeset in 9.5/13, Mundo Sans Pro Regular by iEnergizer/Aptara®, Ltd.
Printed in Great Britain by Ashford Colour Press Ltd.

NOTE THAT ANY PAGE CROSS REFERENCES REFER TO THE PRINT EDITION

This book is dedicated

To John's wife Elizabeth and daughter Katrina
"in gratitude for the precious opportunity to find purpose in all I do".

And to Andrew's parents Roy and Margaret for "showing me
the 'why' in life".

CONTENTS

FOREWORD

For as long as I can remember, identifying and being driven by a clear sense of purpose in business has been extremely important to me.

When I was growing up in the Cheshire railway town of Crewe, my father ran a small grocery wholesale business, supplying small shops and pubs with biscuits, crisps and other confectionery products. He had previously run a shop himself so was all too familiar with the pressures facing such operations. He identified a gap in the market between large producers of biscuits, crisps and confectionery and small stores and pubs who couldn't afford to take the conventional minimum order size of several dozen cases.

A highly principled man and a lay-preacher on Sundays, he taught me three key lessons that formed beliefs I have held throughout my entire career and shaped my decade running Waitrose.

Firstly, he believed very strongly that in the eyes of God, everybody is equal and nobody is better than anybody else. Each person has unique skills and talents, so the task for leaders is to draw these out and make the most of them. He also taught me that we should give help to people where we are able to do so and that, though such acts had altruism at their core, such small acts of kindness can yield huge rewards in the long term.

One day as a teenager I went out delivering food with him and one of our stops was a tiny shop where the owner was just starting up and said he couldn't afford to buy much. My father offered to give him some cases and collect payment later but the shopkeeper said he didn't have enough even for a single case of 24, so my father offered to sell him just half a case, opening a box, taking out half the biscuits and putting them on the shelves.

When we got home, we realised we had given this grocer one packet short. My initial reaction was that it was a trivial oversight; it was late in the day and we should have dinner and go to bed. My father would have none of this however, insisting that agreement had been reached to supply 12 packets and that the extra packet could be significant to this fledgling business shop owner.

We made the round trip to rectify the situation and that commitment to our customer, that effort, was rewarded many times over the forthcoming years. From this tiny shop, the store owner expanded to become one of my father's best customers.

The care and concern my father had shown him was hugely appreciated and he insisted on loyally sticking with my father's business even when his grocery firm grew to become of sufficient size to be supplied directly by a major manufacturer.

I have remembered this throughout my business career and it influenced the Random Acts of Kindness initiative at Waitrose, through which we would do things that people didn't expect.

The initiative, which remains a valued part of Waitrose, was predicated partly on the benefits of making customers feel good about themselves. But there was also strong commercial logic that it should have a long-term benefit for the business. That's exactly how this successful venture turned out. Like many of the ideas and initiatives pioneered in my career at the John Lewis Partnership, its gestation was from the purposeful seeds sown in my thinking by my father.

The John Lewis model is, of course, unique. The Partnership, made up of its people, is essentially managing owners, not employees and therefore the mindset is entirely different to a conventional operation. We didn't tell people what to do. We might ask them but more importantly we needed to engage them in what we needed to do. We needed to ensure everyone understood the purpose of the business and their role within it.

Treating people with respect and everyone being equally important were not only the right things to do but were also good for business, whether the people concerned were on the shop floor or in the boardroom. This also related to our suppliers, customers and the wider communities within which we operated and without which we could not prosper.

My firm belief is that one can have the best strategy in the world, make great decisions about new products and correctly gauge the appetite for new retail space in attractive locations. However, none of those will bear fruit if the cashiers, for example, aren't striking the right tone with customers. It is so easy to lose business like that. So what really matters is how every individual comes to feel key in the business and very much part of the journey.

All of my time in the Partnership was about making people feel that what they did was worthwhile and developing their skills, aptitudes and experience so that together we did a great job commercially. We invested in equal measure in the relationships with our suppliers and then ensured our customers felt good through charitable initiatives and random acts of kindness.

That's what clarity of purpose in business means for me. It is driven by relationships with people, be they employees, customers or people in our supply chain. It harks back to what I learned from my father and together such relationships form the basis of good business in all its forms.

This is fundamentally about creating a purposeful culture, based on strong ethical values and a sound commercial offering. Under the right leadership, these combine to allow people to understand what you are setting out to achieve. This has never been more important for businesses generally and society at large at a time when the entire capitalist system is coming under pressure.

People now are trying to find a different and better way of doing "good" business. If your business has clarity of purpose, based on sound ethical principles, and its leaders and individuals also have clear senses of their own purpose and role, the business will function better and be more resilient to the inevitable forces of the market. It will also be better at attracting top talent, growing customer loyalty and building long-term sustainable success.

There are now a growing set of business models vying for attention in this space. There is also a wider debate about the role of business in society generally, which John and Andrew do not seek to add to here. Instead, based on their collective half century in this arena, working with, advising, observing and commentating on business, this useful and accessible guide outlines how organisations can find, express and benefit from a clear sense of purpose.

How this can be applied, what it means and how it will affect your business, leadership, employees and customer engagement will be different for each business. By providing simple steps to follow and inspiring contributions from a wide range of purposeful leaders, this book allows and encourages readers to think differently about their business approach and role.

I hope "The Power of Purpose" will help your own business and career, as well as be a major contribution to the debate about how purpose can be defined, measured and lived in our businesses and enterprises.

I wish you all the best in your own purposeful journeys.

Lord Mark Price
Former Managing Director of Waitrose

ABOUT THE AUTHORS

John O'Brien

After school and a few years in retail banking, John attended the Royal Military Academy at Sandhurst. He served 10 years as an infantry officer, retiring in 1994 and spent the next 23 years focusing on corporate responsibility and cross-sector partnerships, becoming an established expert in creating significant collaborative, purpose-led initiatives.

For 10 years he was a director of the charity Business in the Community, and held responsibility for the Prince of Wales's personal programmes: creating the Mosaic UK & international youth programmes, leading the Prince's business leadership programme "Seeing is Believing", The Prince's Rural Action Programmes and BITC international.

In his personal capacity, John has created charitable endeavours including the Jubilee Hour campaign for Her Majesty's Diamond Jubilee and Remember WW1 as part of the UK's commemorative period. He is founding patron of the Patchwork Foundation, supporting young people to learn about UK democracy, patron of MPCT, preparing young people for employment, has served as a Trustee of SSAFA, the service welfare charity and as a magistrate specialising in youth courts. He is a Trustee of the Prince of Wales's International Network for Traditional Building, Architecture and Urbanism (INTBAU).

John lives with his wife and daughter in Shropshire.

Andrew Cave

Andrew has been interviewing the world's leading chief executives for more than 20 years. A former Associate City Editor of *The Daily Telegraph*, he has been writing about business and leadership for the newspaper in London and New York since 1996. This is his third book, following *The Secrets of CEOs* and *Billions to Bust and Back*. He lives in Oxford.

The global chief executives and chairmen he has interviewed include Jeff Bezos of Amazon, Larry Ellison of Oracle, John Chambers of Cisco Systems, Lord Browne, formerly of BP, Lakshmi Mittal of ArcelorMittal, Sir Martin Sorrell of WPP Group and former Tesco CEO Sir Terry Leahy.

Andrew also writes regular columns about leadership for *Forbes*, *CityA.M.* and *CorpComms* and *Corporate Reputation* magazines.

ACKNOWLEDGEMENTS

A big thank you goes to One Hundred colleagues, for their support and encouragement and championing ethical purpose as our own business rationale. In particular to Michelle Brassell for keeping One Hundred on track whilst the book was being written, to Alison Bradley for relentless management of the various content and contributors and to Charlotte Turner for her supporting research. To One Hundred's co-founding partners Dave Allen and Roger Partington for the confidence in One Hundred's unique proposition and to Diana Rose, Rose Green, Peter Widdup, Sally Bye and Jenny Poulter for helping One Hundred become a leading purpose agency. Many of the observations, techniques and insights are shared experiences from within the One Hundred "family" for which we are most grateful.

We would also like to thank Narda Shirley, MD of Gong Communications and her team, with Amanda Lyons in particular for managing relationships with contributors, our publishers and promoting our work. Thank you to Eloise Cook at Pearson, for her guidance and input, to create a viable manuscript, and the wider team which has guided the book to the market with such enthusiasm.

Thanks also to Prof David Grayson, who went beyond the call of duty as a contributor to advise generally on its content, and to the 100 participants detailed within who contributed their time to participate in our questionnaire. We are also grateful to members of The Knot network for their involvement in the collective learning experiences that contribute to the book.

This book owes its rich content to the willingness of our interviewees to share their experiences and we are most grateful to them and to Lord Price for his foreword.

ACKNOWLEDGEMENTS

Finally, thank you to our wives, families and friends for their forbearance and support at times when we were not present and for those times where we may have seemed so, but our minds were on a purpose elsewhere.

As for our purpose of complete accuracy, all responsibility for any short-comings is of course ours alone.

John O'Brien
Andrew Cave

INTRODUCTION

People want purpose

People want to work within, buy from, invest with and see businesses that can be believed in. Such businesses have clarity of purpose and place their purpose above profit.

In picking up and reading this book you have already taken the first steps on a purposeful transition to power performance, both personally and within your business.

So what are businesses for? When this question was asked regularly in the first decade of this century, the answer invariably focused on their raison d'être being to return value to their shareholders. Yet, the crisis of 2008 showed the pursuit of shareholder value to have been an expensive mistake for many.

Multi-billion dollar mergers and acquisitions were carried out in its name but soon had to be unwound. Shareholder value was destroyed, not created. Subsequently, demand has grown for companies to demonstrate a reason for being that transcends markets and cycles.

A clearly defined purpose, along with a roadmap of how to fulfil it, is now being recognised by many across all sectors of business as a requisite for success.

Purpose in business is not a new fad. In nineteenth century UK, pioneers such as the Cadbury, Lever, Pilkington and other families developed their own benevolent capitalism approaches. In recent years, sustainability, employee engagement, corporate responsibility and philanthropy programmes have been added to the mix.

But how do businesses, from entrepreneurial start-ups to large global multinationals, not only define their purpose but ensure that it resonates in everything that they do?

What is purpose?

You instinctively know the people and businesses that have "it". In the individual, "it" might be described as a sense of greatness, charisma, force of nature or presence.

In business, "it" tends to be evoked by strong brand integrity and awareness, robust behaviours, public reputation, trust and confidence. Yet such descriptions fall short of expressing the general sense of value and character that surround such businesses. Maybe it is best expressed another way. The X factor upon which such businesses have built their strength and ongoing success, in absolute clarity and belief, is an overriding sense of purpose.

The purpose of a business has little to do with its size, sector, age or nature of ownership. It is a clear understanding of what it is for, which manifests itself in every facet of its leadership and operation.

Just think for a moment about those you most admire and your reasons for doing so. The answers are likely to add up to them being led by a clearly defined sense of purpose that resonates deeply, is proven to be consistent and gives them a strong reputation and position in today's society.

It is purpose that empowers their people, their products and services and their ability to be competitive and capable of achieving their goals. It is what drives their innovations, makes them both iconic and newsworthy, trendsetters in corporate behaviour and aspirational models for new entrepreneurs.

Whether they seek it or not, they wield influence across entire sections of society, change behaviours and, as a consequence, the world. In the same way that purpose empowers them, it is also what you can identify and harness within yourself and your business, empowering your operations and people.

Human advances

If there is one human, rather than technological advance that this century will be marked by, it will be the understanding of how a deeper appreciation of purpose can deliver profound personal, institutional and societal success.

We believe there are three reasons for this.

First, the millennial generation has come of age and their ambition is not generally fuelled by the mating call of the Porsche, excesses based on fat salaries or a need to conform to perceived societal roles or career norms to illustrate their success.

Their world is far less stable or constrained than that of their parents and they look at it completely differently. Empowered through technology, they are deeply attracted to being part of something bigger than themselves, with loyalty to causes and experiences beyond formal political or religious structures. They embrace principles of entrepreneurship in the widest context and are generally optimistic that they matter to the world and in turn want to do things that matter to them.

At the Forbes publishing empire, the company's four strategic pillars of print, digital, brand and technology all live under the mission statement that commits the group to be the pre-eminent champion of entrepreneurs and free market capitalism.

Forbes' chief executive Mike Perlis says:

> *"That purpose comes first. It's a business purpose but it's one that we're very serious about and it makes a lot of sense for Forbes."*

One of Forbes' major programmes is an annual list of the top business people under the age of 30 and Perlis sees clarity of purpose particularly resonating with this demographic.

> *"One of the dynamics we clearly see in the millennials who make up that population is that they want more than just financial reward from their work life. They want to be associated with purpose and impact. It seems that every new*

millennial business plan comes with real attention paid to purpose. Millennials really want to be associated with good work and giving back, and that is clearly reflected in all the business plans we see."

Parents of millennials also have an awakened sense of responsibility and opportunity in the world. Theirs, remember, is the generation of Sir Richard Branson, Steve Jobs, Bono and Bob Geldof.

Why does this matter to your business? Because millennials are your employees and growth market and their parents are your investors, opinion formers and market influencers. To understand them is to understand the way purpose impacts on the people who are important to your business.

The second reason is that the financial crisis exposed the social, economic and financial fault lines in our society, exacerbating the tensions not only between different levels of wealth but also between contrasting motivations.

Many within the so-called middle and professional classes in the UK find themselves struggling to achieve the level of prosperity they witnessed as children. Their certainties of life were based on the model of university education leading to professional employment, property acquisition and a level of quality of life higher than the previous generation. Now, this is by no means guaranteed.

The resulting insecurity means that many people are rejecting traditional ways of working, living and planning their futures. Again empowered by technology, they are adopting new working and living practices with a different work–life balance agenda and giving increased importance to personal and family priorities, interests and hobbies. In many cases, turning the latter into a means of income.

Finally, trust in institutions has waned, with scandals affecting politicians, business, sport, the media and even some high-profile charities. The result is that those with a sense of personal integrity choose to express this in various ways, from engaging in causes, creating campaigns, investing time and money in micro-businesses and other value-driven organisations.

Major corporate brands, such as Virgin, Google and Amazon, that have also developed a strong public persona, have won high levels of public trust, even when they come under attack from the media or politicians. Their sense of purpose has given people something to trust and value.

Our experiences

This book is shaped by our experiences.

For me, John, the purpose of business, and how organisations exhibit it, has long fascinated me. I began my own purposeful journey in military training at Sandhurst and developed thoughts and methodologies further in the charitable and corporate responsibility sector. Now, I lead One Hundred Partners, a purpose consultancy I cofounded, helping businesses put into practice what I have learned.

For me, Andrew, I have also been delving into the motivations of business people for many years in my newspaper interviews with leading chief executives. My previous book *The Secrets of CEOs* was dedicated to uncovering how today's business leaders actually lead. My next step is to look at why they lead, and how their individual beliefs dovetail with the actions they need to take to make their businesses successful and sustainable.

This book's methodology

Our methodology has been two-fold. First, we undertook a survey of 100 leading organisations from around the world to discover their own definitions of purpose, values and vision.

We found that vision and purpose were strongly cited as drivers of decisions, staff and customer engagement, and that a balance is emerging between financial and social drivers of business.

One respondent stated that purpose-led businesses were those that are "driven by a deep understanding of the organisation's mission, vision, and values and look beyond the need to generate profit". Another defined a purpose-powered business as "authentic, with a lived experience felt by everyone". A third stated that when an organisation is powered by purpose "what a business stands for becomes more important than what it sells".

Respondents said that purpose-led businesses are characterised by long-term thinking, a sense of moral compass and honesty. Asked to identify the most important indicators of business success in today's environment, 61% specified the social and environmental impact of business, ahead of profitability (56%) and an innovative and entrepreneurial nature (49%).

An overwhelming majority of participants agreed that clarity of purpose influences an organisation's vision, strategic decision making and staff morale and performances. Two-thirds of respondents saw corporate boards as the most influential shapers of purpose within organisations.

Next, we sought to understand what some of the most purposeful and influential business leaders are doing that is different, powerful and sustaining. Through interviews with leading chief executives, as well as lesser-known but emerging individuals who have also found their purpose and accomplished extraordinary achievements, we looked for insights to allow others to find, refine and empower their purpose, inspire those around them and lead the organisations they care about.

What was the defining moment in their own lives that led these individuals to devote their leadership to inculcating a highly defined sense of purpose in their organisations?

We found that, for these highly driven individuals, purpose transcends pure financial gain, having a far-reaching societal impact. Yet the modern purpose-led leader is no woolly "do-gooder". The business leaders who have contributed to this book are fierce believers in the necessity for revenues, profits, investment and growth. Without a healthy profit base, a purpose-led business cannot thrive.

Purpose and you

What does purpose mean for you and your business? This book will introduce you to a simple route to purpose, which we apply successfully through One Hundred. We aim to demonstrate from a practical rather than theoretical basis the value in purpose. Such value can be measured, in material and monetary success, in social and environmental impact, in personal health and wellbeing.

It is nothing less than the single all-encompassing key to unlocking the potential in individuals and organisations in the twenty-first century.

It is also based on a key contention that, given the expectations of our next generations, financial crisis scandals, austerity, climate change and corruption scandals from sport to governments, what the world needs now, what companies and institutions should seek to develop and what we as individuals have as latent untapped potential, is a greater sense of purpose based on ethical values.

This book will allow you to consider how purpose can become your own powerful driver for change. We will explain why purpose matters to you, your business and your world.

Talking with Richard Branson, he is clear on how the purpose agenda has driven his business success.

> *"Long before the term purpose was used to describe the mission and values of a business, I was building purpose-driven companies. I started my first business, Student Magazine, to give young people a voice to speak out against the Vietnam War and on causes we believed in. The same spirit of striving to make a positive difference is in the DNA of every Virgin business.*
>
> *But this isn't just because building purposeful businesses is the right thing to do – it is also the smart thing to do. Purpose-driven businesses simply run better. They help make employees happier, more engaged, harder working and longer serving. They appeal to growing numbers of customers who care more and more about the purpose*

behind the brand they endorse, rather than just the product or service.

Purpose gives our businesses a competitive edge, a roadmap to guide us, and short and long-term vision. But more than that, it gives us the energy and motivation to continue pushing to make a positive difference to people's lives. Purpose spurs passion, which fans the sparks that light the fires that fuel change. If you are building a business without purpose, not only are you missing the point, but you are most likely missing out on the journey, the excitement – and the profit – too."

With our own purpose of helping others find their purpose within business, we hope to inspire you on this journey.

John O'Brien and Andrew Cave

Chapter 1

Why you need purpose

A fundamental truth

We need to face up to some fundamental truths. You have purchased this book because you are interested in two things: being successful in business and life, and understanding how clarity of purpose can help you achieve that.

However, each and every one of us has different circumstances, responsibilities, interests and aspirations that shape our actions, even the action of purchasing this book. So, even though we hope you will find this book helpful, each of you will find your own path to purpose.

Those differences, of course, sometimes are distinctions that can appear to hamper our progress to success rather than support it. We suggest they are not, and that they are a key part of your life and story.

These factors are everywhere and everyone has them. However, the key to making a genuine difference is the discovery that, rather than being a short-term hindrance, these factors can be part of the chemistry that shapes your life experiences and, in turn, can shape your purpose.

This book needs to be read with that approach to your thinking, about how to apply that way of thinking to your career and business.

A new perspective

How often have you heard successful people tell you that they have learnt more from their failures than successes? In our view, there is no such thing as a wasted experience or a failure from which we cannot learn.

Some of the strongest purpose-led leadership we have come across has been forged by individuals appreciating where purpose has been weak, allowing other negative aspects to prevail. Just as such recognitions become valuable life lessons in our personal lives, they are illustrative of the importance of purpose.

Being in the business of championing and advising others on purpose-driven leadership, we have never before seen so many new and existing leaders looking for clarity, focus and innovative insights to drive successful business with positive societal impact.

Over the past 30 years, new perspectives have emerged on what success and life should be about. Entire industries have disappeared and been replaced by new ones. Old touchstones and certainties that previous generations took for granted have either proved false or all but disappeared.

Purpose in action

The last 10 years in particular have seen the concept of purpose rise as a major influence among leaders across all sectors and around the world. This demand for greater purpose comes from:

- established companies with a need to find new, authentic ways of creating sustainable value across all their stakeholders;

- entrepreneurs wanting to demonstrate a deep sense of personal purpose as they carve out new areas of businesses and social enterprise;

- government agencies looking to create collective communities of purpose-driven people, engaged in civil society;

- individuals looking to make an impact on the people and issues they care about;

- charities and non-government organisations (NGOs) wanting to create clarity around their rationale and the way they operate to deliver enhanced impact.

We have seen purpose successfully applied within all these sectors and this book is applicable across them all, albeit written from a business perspective.

Such clarity of purpose has supported all these demands and proved helpful in all manner of decision making. It has been tailored to today's complex, competitive and changeable environment and it has helped executive teams as well as individuals increase their productivity levels.

Above all, it has moved from a concept to practical activation, rapidly changing expectations, methodologies of delivery and commercial success.

Why purpose matters is akin to questioning the meaning of life and, in many ways, it is just as important. But finding purpose is achievable and it can be the key to unlocking a sense of meaning for individuals and organisations.

This book will bring the finding of purpose within your grasp, allowing you to define the way in which you run your business and exceed expectations.

With ever-increasing demands on personal energy, shortening response times and constant real-time emergent issues requiring solutions, people and businesses can become reactive, responding to life with little time to reflect on the wider implications or to prepare well-thought-out responses. It might seem impossible to find the time to determine the purpose you or your business have, beyond day-to-day survival. However, all of these pressures are the very reason why clarity of purpose becomes all-important.

The demise of shareholder value

Professor David Grayson, head of the Doughty Centre at Cranfield University in Bedfordshire, has been promoting corporate responsibility and meaningful business for over 20 years.

He is convinced that the world's 13,000 business schools need to change their prevailing trend of thinking. He sees the need to turn away from a philosophy which has become entrenched since the first days of globalisation in the 1980s, change their prevailing trend that the purpose of business is simply about maximising shareholder value.

This started back with economists such as Milton Friedman and institutions including the Chicago School of Economics which strove to create a formulaic rigour of thinking as a reaction to the flabby business management structures of the 1950s and 1960s. David Grayson and others are convinced that this has been disastrous. As he says:

"This idea that the purpose of business is solely to maximise shareholder value has been insidious."

He argues that an unflinching and dogmatic reliance on shareholder value has justified many takeovers, mergers and other investment decisions that have been carried out in its name but they have delivered just the opposite, destroying value, rather than creating it.

As a management theory, he says shareholder value has also been pretty poor while, philosophically and ethically, a blind adherence to shareholder value mantra leaves businesses rudderless, since what is deemed to be in the investors' interests can fluctuate widely very rapidly.

That may seem a million miles from the world of Will Butler-Adams, managing director of Brompton Bicycle, whose products are synonymous with city commuters. But he agrees:

> *"There's an obsession in business about shareholder value, and I think it's complete balderdash. Shareholder value is an outcome but it's not an objective. The objective of all business has to be the customer. If you make your customer happy, you add value to their life, whether it is a service or a product. But you won't deliver that if you have grumpy, demotivated staff.*
>
> *"And if you don't make a profit, you're not going to be able to pay your staff very well. You're not going to have money to invest in research and development. If you get everything right, you will have fantastic shareholder value. The problem is that, for some reason, we have a society at the moment in which that is where you start. Well, if you start with shareholder value, if you're not careful it can be tail wagging the dog. You spiral, cut costs and try to deliver short-term shareholder value, which is a false friend."*

David Grayson points back to business philosopher Charles Handy's now famous seminal lecture at the Royal Society for the Arts in London in 1990. The topic was "What Is A Company For?". Handy stressed the need to reevaluate why businesses actually exist. He said:

> *"A company ought to be a community: a community that you belong to, like a village. Nobody owns a village. You are a member and you have rights. Shareholders will become financiers, and they will get rewarded according to the risk they assume, but they're not to be called owners. And workers won't be workers, they'll be citizens, and they will have rights. And those rights will include a share in the profits that they have created."*

Almost three decades later, after the biggest financial crisis in history, Handy's vision is now being recognised and embraced by many as the principles around which to build purpose-driven businesses.

Handy came to the conclusion that it is up to each individual business to work out its own purpose and that optimising shareholder value over the medium to long-term should be the consequence, not the purpose of a well-run business.

Handy was joined in that view nineteen years later by Jack Welch, who as chief executive of American conglomerate General Electric had been closely associated with the shareholder value model of delivering quarter-upon-quarter growth for investors.

Welch declared in the *Financial Times*:

> *"On the face of it, shareholder value is the dumbest idea in the world . . . Shareholder value is a result not a strategy . . . Your main constituencies are your employers, your customers and your products."*

Dave Packard, cofounder of IT group Hewlett-Packard, grasped this issue early on.

> *"Many people assume wrongly that a company exists simply to make money. While this is an important result of a company's existence, we have to go deeper and find the real reasons for our being. As we investigate this, we inevitably come to the conclusion that a group of people get together and exist as an institution that we call a company so that they are able to accomplish something collectively that they could not accomplish separately. They make a contribution to society, a phrase which sounds trite but is fundamental."*

A "contribution ethic"

This motivation to have a "contribution ethic" is not something that has only just emerged. It has been a strong motivating force for many business people over more than a century, as the Cadbury, Lever and Pilkington families in the UK demonstrated.

Since the 1970s, however, the dominance of the shareholder value thinking relegated such ethical thinking to the fringes, being seen more as a quirky concept. Perhaps it was capable of being successful in the hands of maverick business leaders, but not necessarily something that could be embraced or applied collectively by all.

The good news is that it never went away as a guiding light of some companies. For example, founded in 1668, Merck is the world's oldest pharmaceutical and chemicals group. With the founding family remaining the majority owner of the publicly listed corporate, one could argue that it illustrates clearly the link between sustainable success and clarity of purpose, building 300 years of value in all senses of the word.

Its company president (1925–1950) W. Merck maintained that the medicine the company created was for patients, not profits. More than 300 years later, in 1987, in keeping with this core value, his successors decided to give away for free the drug Mectizan, which cures river blindness, an affliction in a number of developing countries.

In 2016, Merck announced its new purpose was to "Prepare society for a new era of humans living 100 healthy years".

What an extraordinary, bold, aspirational and engaging purpose, and one that will be brought to life through what the company describes as the "WE100" movement, aimed at raising awareness of healthy living, all the way from childhood to 100 years.

With its motto "Young for old. Old for young", WE100 will coordinate concrete actions to help prepare society for humans living 100 healthy years. Nowhere does this slogan talk about selling products or maximising profits. It defines clearly the purpose as its cause and it roots its purpose in something we can all be interested in.

This thinking is now spreading because it is now being recognised as the antidote to the failure of alternative business models that have had profoundly damaging effects. To survive, even to prosper, is simply no longer seen as enough.

The legacy of a cause

One of the over-riding influences we see being acknowledged within purpose-driven leaders is their personal motivation for legacy. As individuals, they and we generally want such a legacy, the thinking of leaving "a footprint in the sands of time". Where we see we can achieve this with the help and companionship of the like-minded, in an organisation we can feel committed to, then so much the better.

Many would say that to give purpose to our lives we need to associate ourselves with a cause. To that we add that such causes do not have to be seen traditionally as the exclusive property of charities. Rather, such causes can include creating a business with value in all senses of the word, for the world at large and is noble in itself.

David Grayson at Cranfield University argues that "all business should not have the same purpose". He states:

"On the contrary . . . it is up to each business to do the serious work, to define for themselves: 'what is our purpose?'" Grayson cites Blueprint for Better Business and the B-Corp movement as two examples of organisations which are active in promoting business to define their own purpose.

Although some people might argue that a business purpose is not a cause, we challenge them to redefine their own thinking about what both the language and business stands for. That is the point.

A long-term outlook

Paul Polman, chief executive of food and personal care products group Unilever, has been a leader in taking a longer-term approach to business where other metrics, as well as shareholder value, are used to measure and denote business success.

One of his early actions at the company was to abandon its quarterly reporting of financial results because he believes that reporting on a long-term basis will engender a long-term outlook. He has moved the employee share scheme's goalposts from three to five years for the same reason. For

Polman, the driving force has to be alignment with customers. If that is successful, he says shareholder returns surely will follow.

"The best businesses understand their consumer intimately. They are real people with complex lives and concerns. That's why the market for responsible, purpose-driven brands is growing so rapidly. There's a massive return for companies on these social investments. We need to step up and deliver not in a half-hearted way or by simply paying lip service to the 'green' lobby but through genuinely purpose-driven brands that answer a real need."

John Fallon, chief executive at educational publisher Pearson (publishers of this book, incidentally), is pragmatic, understanding that pension funds and other shareholders have their own need for returns to deliver for their policyholders. But he insists:

"The way you create sustainable value for shareholders over time is to meet an important need and to do it well. The purpose of Pearson as a company is to help more people to progress in their lives by giving them access to better quality of learning and helping them to translate that into better career prospects and opportunities.

"That's driven by a view that education will emerge over the next 20 years to be a big opportunity in the same way as health, clean water, the environment and feeding and clothing people. It's a fundamental need in an increasingly knowledge and skills-based economy that people having the ability to learn and carry on learning throughout their working lives is going to be something of increasing value.

"Our purpose is to help meet that need in a way that's more effective and deliver a better return on investment for individuals, the state and society. If we do that well, then over time we will create a faster-growing and more profitable business. We're a profit-making organisation. Profits don't define us but they certainly sustain us and the best way to have a profitable and sustainable business is to do what we do better. That's the way we would define our purpose."

We have an inherent human ability for individuals and collectively as organisations to have clarity of thought, to be able to make wise decisions and respond meaningfully to circumstances. However, this provides only part of the answer to motivating, leading and delivering.

The identification of purpose as a unifying all-encompassing belief within a business greatly enhances every measure of whether a business is effective. Most importantly, the resulting reduction in stress and concern, with deep instilled confidence in the role one is playing, leads to greatly enhanced employee satisfaction and results.

Purpose for the individual

While this book is focused on empowering business, we need to understand why purpose matters to individuals and to societies, in order to understand its power in business.

As an individual, there are some main factors to understand:

- What we inherently feel as humans. These are consistent influences across history and form undeniable truths for individuals, affecting deep-rooted motivations and behaviours.

- How we as individuals are affected by what we do and how we spend our time.

These two influences affect the way a business operates because your stakeholders, staff, customers, suppliers and shareholders, although apparently different and motivated by varying interactions with the business, are all human and have the same inherent influencers.

A critical aspect of this understanding is that we all want to feel we belong, to consider that we are connected to those around us by common values and interests. This desire to belong makes us do extraordinary things. We might change the way we talk or dress or take up practices that are new to us, in order to be acceptable within a wider group.

This human trait has been a powerful driver of twentieth century culture, with the adoption of branded products bestowing a sense of belonging to certain consumer demographics. Bizarrely, in a world dominated by individualism, where high-tech products and fashion strive to create a sense of the personal, brands can take the form of movements, becoming universal to be seen to belong. Adopting such brands bestows an acceptability on adopters and the motivation for such adoption is key to a corporate clarity of purpose.

Another key human trait is a desire to feel a part of something bigger than oneself. We feel drawn to become fans of sporting teams or rock bands, we want to sign up to global campaigns, build followings on social media platforms and join mass mobilised protests. These are attempts to amplify our voices by adding them to hundreds and thousands of others.

When we see our apparent importance to something bigger than ourselves, we feel bigger ourselves. When it comes to encouraging purpose in businesses, leaders need to create the same sense of joining and amplification.

How we spend our time is the other big factor in determining our ability to harness the power of purpose within business. What occupies most of our time inevitably affects us most, our piece of mind, our health and those around us.

For many, work is dominant, whether a househusband, business person, charity volunteer or public servant and regardless of remuneration. So it also becomes important that the value sets of the companies that people work for are in line with their own clearly defined life purpose.

One of the most recognised purpose-focused leaders is Unilever's chief executive Paul Polman, who told *The Guardian* in 2013:

> *"I know we all have our jobs but that has to come from a deeper sense of purpose. You have to be driven by something. Leadership is not just about giving energy; it's unleashing other people's energy, which comes from buying into that sense of purpose. But if that purpose isn't strong enough in a company, if the top doesn't walk the talk, then the rest will not last long. The key thing for CEOs is to make that a part of your operating model."*

Polman has put purpose at the heart of Unilever, dictating its social and environmental impact around the world.

At Virgin Group, moreover, Sir Richard Branson, states:

> *"It's incredibly important to have purpose. This is something I have always held true in life and in business. I didn't start Virgin to make money; instead I wanted to make a positive difference in people's lives. Why? Because I thoroughly believe that we should do everything within our power to make the world a better place for generations to come."*

Purpose versus corporate social responsibility

Building upon existing research and then interviewing senior business leaders and engaging with social entrepreneurs, emerging disrupters and leaders of sustainability and corporate responsibility activities, we see that purpose has moved to the centre stage of business in a way that mere corporate social responsibility (CSR) strategies have never managed.

We need to ensure that people understand purpose is not CSR. It isn't a "green" sustainability plan either. It is something much more profound that we will show gives you the opportunity to think much bigger about your impact in the world than choosing what paper or energy to use.

Nobody denies that the pioneers of corporate philanthropy, CSR and the sustainability agenda did valuable work in preparing the way over the last 20 years. John spent 10 years leading such initiatives at the Prince of Wales's charity Business in the Community, in which many of those interviewed in this book have also played prominent roles.

However, many will acknowledge that, although good things were and still are championed by such organisations, it also has allowed for some more cynical companies simply to see it as another "agenda item" often placed in boxes or "silos", with departments to run CSR programmes or foundations and community projects far removed from the practical management of the business.

John believes that all that effort on CSR and environmental sustainability was critical in changing business behaviour and society for the better, but it has, effectively, become, a minimum standard, almost a means of minimising adverse public attention from mainstream business activities.

Banks were illustrative of this and shamed so publicly in the financial crisis. They have proven the disconnect with grand philanthropic and community activities on the one hand but where they could still have internal remuneration incentives that drove immoral and illegal behaviours elsewhere.

Public-facing mission statements and awards for CSR were, in effect, irrelevant to the way that many companies actually managed their business activities. When the financial crisis hit and such fig-leaf activity became obvious, there was a general call for an agenda best described as being capable of "profits with purpose".

This began a recognition that the two are far from incompatible and, indeed, they are vital to each other. However, with sustainability's environmental and social challenges causing ever-growing stakeholder demands and governments seen as incapable of influencing such behavioural change, enlightened business leaders realised that the key was not simply profits with purpose but rather "profits from purpose". That's the mantra now for fundamental change in business leading to greater sustainable success.

Butler-Adams of Brompton Bicycle adds:

> *"We have to make profits. You won't fulfil your purpose if you're not successful and profitable. You could have the best purpose in the world but you won't affect anyone. That's why profits are so important. We've got to be competitive, aggressive and innovative to fulfil our purpose because purpose is only of any value if it affects things and makes change happen.*
>
> *"If you have wonderful purpose and affect nothing, you have delivered nothing; there's legacy. What have you done? You've wasted your time. You can't run a business that doesn't make good profits because you need profit to take risks and to innovate."*

Why a business exists

Definitions for business purpose are various but, quite simply, we would argue a purpose is "the reason for operating, its positive relevance to the world and its ability to inspire people". It is important to state this clearly and to understand it, because sometimes people confuse this with the means of doing something, or what they are doing.

Purpose, quite simply, is **why** a business exists: it is what we aim to achieve in the world and for people generally, rather than how we aim to achieve it. This clarity is doubly important in business when many can get stuck on process or the mechanics of existing services and products.

In reality, to purpose-power your business, you must place purpose before the means, as one would with horses before a cart. The means of achieving your aim only become clear after the purpose is. This shouldn't surprise us because in general life we always have a purpose when we start to do something. We tend not to start to walk unless we know where we are heading. In leading a more mature existing business, as opposed to a start-up, it can be harder to draw this distinction because day-to-day business often gets in the way.

But you can rectify this.

 In our 150 questionnaire and interview responses, alongside our 50 or so client-based experiences, we have found that the concept of purpose-powered business is defined broadly under two themes:

- The first was where such clarity of purpose was being used as its vision, to drive decisions, staff and customer engagement.

- The second is where its conscious development was as a direct result of wanting to create the right balance between financial and social drivers, effectively a development from traditional CSR.

Here are some responses.

> *"Business that is driven by a deep understanding of the organisation's mission, vision, and values and that looks beyond the need to generate profit."*

"A purpose-powered business is authentic, with a lived experience that is felt by everyone."

"What a business stands for becomes more important than what it sells."

"A business that is able to reconcile the tension between the bottom line and the wider responsibilities of business."

"Purpose-driven business is characterised by both intent and impact. The intent to use business as a tool for societal change and a deep understanding of – and interest in – the whole impact of that business."

These are all helpful, but we believe a much simpler question should be the starting point for your thinking.

Why are you in business?

So let us start by stating it very clearly. To have absolute clarity of your business's purpose is to know why you are in business. In our model of purposefulness, your business is not powered by simply thinking you are in business to make money. Rather it is powered by the fact that, with a bigger purpose, money will be made and that money will allow you to grow even bigger with purpose.

Jørgen Knudstorp, chief executive of Lego, is very clear in his thinking:

"While we need to make money, the Lego Group has a deeper purpose than that. Our purpose is to make a difference in children's lives by giving them wonderful play experiences, and bringing this experience to every child on the planet. Money is like oxygen to a body, but none of us sit in this room to breathe the air; we sit in this room to fulfil a purpose with our lives. Making money is the entry ticket to fulfilling that purpose."

At online gifting marketplace Notonthehighstreet.com, chief executive Simon Belsham says the company's purpose goes back to its foundation in 2006 by advertising executives Holly Tucker and Sophie Cornish. Tucker was weaving craft products in her spare time, selling at craft fairs. The duo wanted a more regular way of selling their products and decided to create a marketplace for the best, most creative small businesses that they could find.

Belsham says:

> *"Their purpose was connecting the best small creative businesses with the world, and that purpose has remained with us ever since. It's on the wall in our headquarters and all the words are thought through. Purpose is something we're incredibly passionate about.*
>
> *"Notonthehighstreet.com was founded 10 years ago with a very strong purpose and it's at the heart of everything we do. For me, purpose manifests itself in every part of the business, whether it's the products we sell, the culture of the business, the values of the team and the way we work together as a team and the way we market the business and the brand."*

? In recent years, the emergence of purpose both as an agenda advocated by not-for-profits focused on major corporate engagement and the desire in such companies to attempt to replicate shining examples has led to a risk of it becoming a short-lived corporate trend.

Putting responsibility for purpose into a brand or marketing team is not the correct starting point. Increasingly, it is becoming clear that a relevant, effective purpose, one that informs, motivates and engages all stakeholders, needs to be driven from and by the very top leadership of a company. This is because purpose is not a mere message but the very essence of why your business exists. It should guide all aspects of your culture, decision making, understanding, practices and processes.

One question is how to define purpose, compared to other business buzzwords such as mission, vision and values.

Purpose compared with mission, vision and values

A mission describes where the focus of a business is, in terms of specialism. A good starting point is simply to clarify what is different from the well-established labels already used to describe organisational direction. If you accept that purpose equals why, then the distinction becomes clearer.

The purpose or why of Walgreens Boots Alliance is to "help people across the world lead healthier and happier lives". That's why the company is in business.

Edwin Booth is chairman of Booths Supermarkets, the upmarket food stores chain in the north of England, with a huge reputation for quality in all it does. Talking with Booth, you get a real sense of family values. It was founded by his great great grandfather in 1847 with a stated purpose to sell the best-quality goods in shops staffed by first-class assistants.

> *"Purpose is absolutely vital and even more vital is making sure that it is understood by everybody within an organisation. It's not enough to have a purpose fully understood by a strategic board. It has to be disseminated throughout the entire enterprise and repeated so that people live and breathe it. You have to continually talk about the idea.*
>
> *"Our idea was centered on high-quality service, quality interaction with quality people, care for the people working for the business. In expressing this, one has to be careful it doesn't become too corporate in the sense that it becomes pure process. It has to be part of a culture, a way of thinking and an attitude."*

At Pearson, chief executive John Fallon feels similarly about the company's historical commitment to people:

> *"One of the factors that keeps people here is that they buy in to the vision and purpose. Most people who come to Pearson say it's a very purpose-driven organisation. Even before Pearson was involved in education, there was something about the culture of the company and a belief in the family that started it that business has to work more effectively for society.*
>
> *"There's a story about Pearson as a construction company in the late nineteenth century when the grandson of the founder was using ground-breaking technology to build railroad tunnels under the Hudson River in New York. They had to send divers down to drill deep underneath the water and he would go down personally to test them. And when they were building a railroad across Mexico, they would build a small hospital for the community every 50 or 100 miles. Those stories have*

become part of the culture of this company. Our values are about being brave, imaginative, decent and accountable."

 A vision is what an organisation wishes to be like in some years' time. It suggests something on the horizon towards which it will move.

Ericsson, the Swedish communications company, defines its vision as being "the prime driver in an all-communicating world". It can include customer type, level or scale. Its aim is to provide focus for management and staff.

And values show how an organisation's culture should make it behave; they act as a behavioural compass.

Coca-Cola's stated values include having the courage to shape a better future, leveraging collective genius, being real, and being accountable and committed.

Overall, the understanding you have to have is that purpose is about performance. It is a key driver for just about every aspect of your potential business needs from attracting investment to recruiting new young talent.

Purpose matters because it drives every aspect of commercial growth and success. In 2015, the Havas "Meaningful Brands Index" stated that brands perceived as "meaningful" are benefiting from 46% higher share of wallet, based on 300,000 people across 34 countries.

If one focuses on stakeholders, a clear focus establishes a stronger definition on the marketplace and drives innovation in products and services, building deeper customer and stakeholder relationships. When such purpose is clearly ethical and based on sustainable credentials, it opens up a world of opportunity to meet the demands of a very changed society.

Lord Browne, the former chief executive of BP, rang the death knell in 2015 when he declared "CSR is dead". He advocated that businesses needed to engage more radically with society. Companies, he said, should stop trying to do just the minimum by causing less harm or "offsetting" it through other projects. Instead, they should start to act like responsible citizens, becoming a genuine force for positive change.

In 2015, Unilever stated that the company's sustainable living brands accounted for half of its growth in the previous year. That becomes a substantial signal of a change lever of customer expectation.

Better decision making

Purpose manifests itself in business in the way that decisions are made. When one is clear about a business and its purpose, decisions that in the past might have been ambiguous, or may have created anxiety or uncertainty, become much clearer.

Clarity of purpose creates clarity of decision making. Clearer decisions lead to more confident decisions, which in turn mean more engaged stakeholders, rigorous self-determined values, meaningful brand values and customer loyalty.

(?) Professional services company EY transformed its own sense of purpose and undertook a company survey in 2014, which showed that a staggering 87% of its questioned business leaders believed that companies with a purpose beyond simply maximising profits performed better.

Our own research and interviews bear this out in the way decisions are made within purposeful businesses.

Simon Belsham says:

> *"Our purpose is absolutely core to the commercial and economic model of Notonthehighstreet.com. Our purpose delivers the decisions we make about the company."*

This is confirmed by Ben Fletcher, former managing director of Boots Opticians, who thinks it is really relevant in how you manage business situations. He recalls how Boots decided to remove peroxide, which is common in the care of some older contact lenses, requiring the mixing of a peroxide solution.

> *"We noticed that, whilst the prevalence of it was not large, on occasion consumers would inadvertently put the peroxide in their eye and burn the cornea. It looked awful and could last about 40 hours. It didn't do permanent damage, but it was pretty nasty when it happened.*
>
> *"We actually looked and said: 'Why are we putting customers in this position when, with the product technology these days, they don't actually need it?' We decided to remove peroxide and work with customers who regularly ordered those types of*

contact lenses to explain. We would say to them that there's a better solution that actually would mean that you'll never run this risk. It kept our purpose at the forefront rather than accepting what was the norm."

Alison Platt, chief executive of property services group Countrywide and a former managing director of BUPA, says:

"There is more to people wanting to give themselves at work than simply to receive a salary. Enabling our business to connect our people with your purpose and the difference they are making to the lives of the customers we serve is a route to being better differentiated and more productive. It's enormously enabling in terms of the priority of our strategy.

"Why do we exist? We're here to create value through making a difference to people in terms of the roof over their head. We cannot, as individuals at every level, create returns for shareholders. But we can create differentiation by making a difference in the area of people's lives where our business operates that is putting people and property together.

"People at every level of this business can ask themselves what they're doing to enable that to be as good as it can be. In terms of strategy, purpose brings clarity because our start point is always: is this consistent with our purpose and does it enable us to better achieve it? Clarity of purpose is also critical in defining investments, merger and acquisition targets, development areas and the key performance indicators we set for the business."

It was Brandpie, a branding consultancy whose cofounders founded One Hundred, that helped professional services firm Ernst & Young define its new identity and purpose as EY. It developed a stated purpose of "building a better working world". EY has since striven to centre all its activities around that single stated sense of purpose. It states:

"Purpose could connect all parts of the societal ecosystem . . . Companies with a clearly expressed purpose might directly contribute to a new level of joined-up action from business, governments, NGOs and entrepreneurs."

Dave Allen of Brandpie says:

"My purpose has always been to help organisations find that idea that, simply expressed, unlocks human potential and really excited people and helps the business get a sense of direction. It's about the process around which you get people to align around an idea. The key moment is when the leadership of an organisation signs off an idea and aligns around it. If that doesn't take place, then nothing happens."

At Virgin, Sir Richard Branson is absolutely clear in his definition and publicly champions it:

"The purpose of business purpose is to both run better companies and to run companies better. Purpose-driven companies make a positive difference in the lives of their employees, their communities and the world.

"At Virgin, we focus on diversity and inclusion, giving back to communities, and many important global, environmental and social issues from climate change to LGBT rights to ending the war on drugs. But that's only half the story. Purpose-driven companies run better. Employees are happier. Being purpose-driven also aligns your business better with your customers."

Sustainable success

The experience of the chief executives we interviewed, backed by our consulting work and the research of a further 100 respondents, shows a growing recognition that the development of clarity of purpose gives a stronger basis for long-term sustainable success and long-term profits.

These leaders recognise also that for a brand to have the value of purpose, it must include within it a strong sense of its social and environmental impact. This goes well beyond providing the best products and services, recognising that a corporate capable of being sustainable has to play a part in tackling social and environmental challenges that concern society. Companies can no longer do business in isolation from the worries of the rest of the world.

Jon Bolton, CEO of Liberty Steel and formerly managing director of a number of Tata Steel Businesses, says:

> *"If you're going to communicate what you want to do, particularly in a big industrial organisation in the steel industry, it has to be simple, it has to be really clear and it has to engage. It is difficult to engage with people on a purely financial level. You engage by identifying common purpose".*

> *"In the steel industry, there's been a huge amount of restructuring and if you're going to achieve a constructive and positive outcome you've got to ensure that the different stakeholders are all pointing in the same direction. The causes that bind people together generally are employment and community; fundamentally these can help form the basis for a sense of common purpose between employees, unions, politicians and the employer. As a business leader achieving this can be difficult and potentially hard to reconcile with the goals and objectives of the company that you're part of. But nevertheless, it can be done."*

? Educational publisher Pearson has gone through an extensive process of organisational change where purpose has been instrumental in clarifying the business focus. Its stated purpose is an ambitious one that requires every Pearson product and service to have a "measurable impact on improving peoples' lives through learning".

It recognises that some services could potentially generate short-term profit but not necessarily meet the goals of customers and that, in the long term, this would erode trust and be bad for continued sustainable commercial success. Therefore, linking products back to its purpose continually helps to ensure the relevance of their products to customers.

John Fallon says:

> *"We judge ourselves and invite others to judge us not by the products that we make but by their impact on learners."*

With all this in mind, companies now strive to find out what they stand for as much as the next thing to sell. As we cherish experiences as much as products or services themselves, we demand to know a company's values to check that they are in line with our own. This doesn't just apply to consumer business, because a values-led, purpose-driven business will also appreciate that its own reputation is dependent upon its suppliers. Why would employees who have chosen to work in a purposeful business be interested in working with, supplying or being supplied by a company lacking similar values?

Public trust

Negative "push" factors have also made it imperative for business leaders to understand why they need to change. The financial crisis of 2008 has left a deep lack of general trust. Rebuilding this is an enormous task that could take a generation.

GlobeScan, the impact research company, for over two decades has been assessing and surveying people around the world on the way they view companies and the impact of companies in society. It says that, collectively and generally, businesses have not managed to re-earn or maintain the public's trust.

When one company does something abhorrent, the general levels of trust in all companies are affected. In comparison, with the scientific community and non-government organisations, trust in businesses remains at a low.

A friend and collaborator of One Hundred is Sir Tim Smit, the serial entrepreneur behind the Eden Project in Cornwall and various other initiatives around the world. He sees this as a major factor.

> *"I think the most important thing in any organisation, and it's the same for a single person as it is for an organisation, is if people can know they can trust your handshake.*

> *"If they know that you are kind and will never knowingly be cruel, if they know that you do not fear being disliked so you will be straight and say what needs saying, you're halfway there already. These are actually pure values. Old-fashioned they may be, but we think the most important modern value is the rediscovery of the old one of trust."*

Companies must recognise the need to make efforts to be much better at communicating their purpose, how this drives their business behaviour and decision making and, subsequently, their value to society at large.

One issue is that, although generations X and Y are much more likely than their forebears to punish companies they see as having acted irresponsibly, it is rarer for consumers to do the opposite, rewarding responsible businesses by switching to buying their products and advocating their "good behaviour". This is, perhaps, a human trait of being more willing to complain but it naturally creates a reactive approach among companies trying to manage negative stories rather than perhaps setting out to promote an inspiring vision of the impact of their business.

Carol Burke, managing director of Unipart Manufacturing Group, says:

"Philosophically, I believe life is not just about you as a person; you have to be involved in something much bigger. Anything you do has to be about other people and the wider human race. My career has always been driven by that.

"We're involved in creating wealth and making money – all the kinds of things that have a bad name. But beneath that, it's about involving all the company's people in our purpose. That's the trick, really. Often there's a disconnect between the purpose of a board and shareholders and the purpose of the shop floor. But giving everybody a sense of common purpose gives you a sense of shared destiny. You don't have to be continually trying to convince everyone of what you're trying to do because you have that shared sense of purpose."

Consumer behaviour

In 2015, Havas Media undertook a brand study of what they term "meaningful brands". The results were significant, showing that such businesses and brands can increase their "Share of Wallet" by seven times and on average gain 46% more Share of Wallet than those identified as being less so.

It went on to reveal that such brands outperform the stock market by 133%, with the top 25 scorers delivering an annual return of nearly 12% – 6.7 times that of the STOXX 1800 stock index.

This survey, significant by any standards because of its reach and scale, showed how people's quality of life and wellbeing connects with brands at both a human and business level. It assessed 1,000 brands with 300,000 people in 34 countries, and ranged over 12 different industries.

Furthermore, the performance of marketing KPIs set by top "meaningful brands" can grow at twice the rate of those set by lower scoring meaningful brands. For example, for every 10% increase in meaningfulness, a brand can increase its purchase and repurchase intent by 6% and price premiums by 10.4%.

This statistically proves that a brand's meaningfulness is a key driver of KPI's success. Essentially, by conventional standards by which investors will measure success and ROI, such purpose-driven brands are proving it translates into performance.

? Apparent in all of this is the fact that we are all now conscious of what we are identified with, via our purchasing. Many of us adopt certain brands as part of our identity, illustrating everything from our eco credentials in the car we drive to our views on ethical investment in terms of where we bank.

Talent attraction

If you take on board the significance of the way in which millennials now think about business, enterprise, brands and their work, it will be no surprise that talent attraction goes up a notch when businesses with a clear ethical purpose enter the market.

In this book you will read illustrations of where the culture of such attraction manifests itself in all manner of employee behaviour, from the extreme of having the corporate logo tattooed through to less seemingly extreme but nevertheless significant, commitments to the businesses.

The best minds, actually regardless of age, want to work on meaningful work in places where they are with like-minded people, on a purpose that they feel proud about and which their skills are best equipped for. In fostering purposeful practices, essentially creating the culture, you will be facilitating the opportunity to bring out the very best of people.

Once you have your talent, it is also about how purpose encourages them as a powerful performance catalyst. Clarity of purpose is proven not just to enhance morale and the workplace culture and trust, but it is also a powerful initiator of innovation.

What we see is that businesses with a clear purpose are far more questioning and they encourage their employees to constantly question whether products and services meet their purpose and even management themselves. If you constantly have something to focus back on to, the purpose, it can, in the same way as it clarifies decision making generally, be used as a means of encouraging new, innovative creative thinking.

A lot of our work is about boiling down the apparent complex back to simplicity of purpose and then asking a radical question, such as "What would happen if your current product raw material no longer existed – how would you still achieve your purpose?" Or "What would happen if we no longer had an office in such a place, how would we still achieve our purpose?"

The combination of talent and an environment to encourage such thinking is a key part of why purpose matters.

Chapter summary

In this chapter you have seen that purpose should matter in the following ways:

- **For your business:** purpose will motivate staff, build clarity of decision making, create a collective sense of value within the business and create a brand and business with which customers will wish to have long-term relationships. It will build long-term mutual benefit.

- **For you as an individual:** purpose will motivate you, provide clarity in your efforts, decision making and sense of worth. It will bring you into alignment with what you, personally, want to be associated with as your personal legacy.

- **For your world:** purpose will drive external engagement, it will create positive impact on those who your business affects and interacts with, building reputation and recognition of the business as a positive influence in the world.

Although the next chapter will look at how you find purpose in business, at this point some reflection will be useful. The following questions and diagrams are designed to assist you in that. If you ask yourself the simple questions below, you should be able to gain a clearer sense of how purpose matters to you, how it can influence the way your business operates and the world you occupy.

Your thinking and interests have to rest at the core of each of these sets of questions and, effectively, should end up as a much clearer understanding at the end.

1. What do you love doing? Answer in terms of working in a team, creative thinking, meeting people, etc. Identify the type of things you really like within any of your roles to date and understand why you do.

2. What would you regret not having done, when looking back on your life? Assess the type of things that might affect your working aspirations, such as "I wish I had travelled more" or "I wish I had been in a more creative world". These factors will shape your thinking around the business environment where your own sense of purpose will feel most aligned.

3. Who do you want to work with? Think about the type of people, their characteristics, style, interests, etc. This will help you see yourself in a work environment with like-minded people.

Here is a simple diagram that attempts to show people the perfect combination for a purposeful person in a purposeful role. If you can answer the questions above and populate the diagram below, you are on your way.

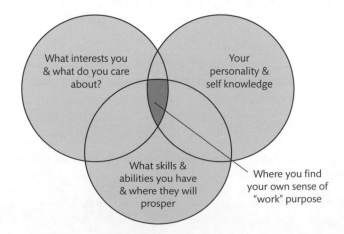

Ask yourself these questions about you in your business:

?   **1.** What type of business do you want to be in? How will your previous answers be reflected through the nature of the business you are in? Does it offer you the opportunity, environment and people to work in an area that will interest you, where your skills and personality will be a positive contribution?

2. What is your role within the business? Does the role you have, or can aspire to, afford you the opportunity to make a purposeful contribution?

3. Does your business purpose align with your own? Ask yourself if the nature of the purpose of your business (however clearly or unclearly currently defined) meets your aspirations as a purpose you can be aligned with. You can prosper with purpose only if both are aligned. The so called "sweet spot" is illustrated below:

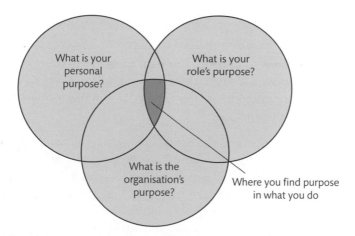

?   This diagram, and the point of your thinking where you can find alignment between all three, is the starting point for the next chapter: "How to find your purpose".

Personal purpose statements

In asking you to assess your own purpose, reflecting upon your life experiences, it is natural and helpful if people wish to create for themselves a succinct explanation of their purpose. Each of us will reflect that differently. Indeed, some people may not wish to be quite so specific, but as illustrative statements here are ours, which we hope will give you some inspiration.

John's purpose

John's purpose is to help people realise the maximum of their potential.

Even before he realised this was his purpose, John was attracted to roles that allowed him to achieve this. He sees himself as having facilitated this purpose through his charitable work, setting up youth mentoring schemes, international leadership programmes, his commercial activities encouraging and advising business leaders and, in his days as an army officer, encouraging young soldiers in their own careers.

He sees this as the golden thread that runs through all he has done across so many different roles.

Andrew's purpose

Andrew's purpose is to discover and elicit truths in an opaque world, rebutting falsehoods and fostering understanding. He strives to do this through curiosity, questioning and writing. This motivates him and is intrinsic to everything he does.

Andrew's career choices and the nature of his writing and journalism reflect this and are illustrative of how it has evolved over the years. It is visionary but aspirational and action-orientated, as well as reflecting his particular personal characteristics that make him a success at what he does.

In writing your own reflective statement, you must use your own language and be true to what you do, rather than what you think people may wish to hear or any particular buzzwords. It needs to reflect the essence of what excites you in all aspects of your life. It can also be helpful to share a purpose statement with one or two trusted people to gain their genuine feedback. Once you have it, if it feels right, you can rest assured it will be right.

Chapter 2

Find your purpose

Introduction

At the end of this book, you will be able to do something that many find impossible after a lifetime of effort. This is possible because we share not only our personal experience, but also that of many other purpose-driven leaders and their experience of having created such clarity of purpose and, in particular, found purpose through business.

We have observed it in others, and over many years have witnessed it, supported it and activated it on this proven pathway. By reading and reflecting on each chapter, completing your own self-assessment and business assessment, you will be able to move through a set of actions to realign your thinking in a purposeful way.

We want to take you on the path of purpose-driven leadership, whether it is to lead yourself as a start-up entrepreneur or to lead a multinational by reigniting or creating a purpose-driven agenda. In doing this, we will be doing nothing less than getting you to look at changing your view of the world and the world's view of you. It is what we have termed "activating purpose for good"™.

This is a bold statement, but the research we have carried out found a deep hunger for purpose in business. Some 81% of respondents said they view themselves as very purpose-powered, though only 60% would describe their organisation in the same way. As many as 86% felt that the rise of organisations examining their purpose will have a positive impact on key global issues such as climate change, poverty and resource depletion, with over half feeling that it would be of significant impact.

This book is designed to be bold in its assumptions about you, what you want to achieve and the impact you want to have on those around you. Our process has been applied in all manner of circumstances and across various roles and industries, including the medical, scientific and academic fields with major corporations, international and domestic charitable campaigns, new product developments, government initiatives and social purpose businesses.

In the last chapter you considered some key questions that form the first part of your transition to understand why purpose matters to you, the business and the world.

Such personal purpose definition starts before the organisational pathway and is an overarching summary of what you are uniquely capable of creating and how your capability can help the organisation achieve its own purpose.

We believe most people want to create something that is valuable for others, and then they want others to use what's been created. This kind of contribution provides its own intrinsic rewards, described in terms like integrity or satisfaction with a job well done.

Furthermore, if you can demonstrate how your contribution helps an organisation achieve its goals, you can make yourself even more valuable at a time when so much else can seem uncertain. This is a step change from suggesting that the point of the business or your role in it is simply to maximise shareholder value and investor exit values.

The exit mentality

To get you thinking about the business context let's consider the key issue of the "exit" mentality.

The propensity to consider the exit strategy from a business, often before a business has even been started, is driven by the requirement for raising investment. However, it has, as a result, acted as a second distraction, alongside the shareholder value model, from actually understanding the purpose of business – and, by default, the business of purpose.

Timothy Melgund, chief executive of stationery and art materials retailer Paperchase, who led a management buyout of the company in 1996, says:

"We always take the long-term view. There's a strange view that you're not a proper entrepreneur if you don't sell your business every few years. I just do not understand that. Surely, it's about trying to create lasting value for all the stakeholders in the business: suppliers, your employees, shareholders and your customers. If you're trying to build a brand, you need to get that clarity of vision and clarity of ownership that people want to maintain their relationships with.

"Our four values are creativity, innovation, high quality and value for money. Those are the four things we never ever let go of. It means you're always pushing out. In the end, people do things for us that they would never dream of doing for anybody else. And that gives us a gap between us and the rest of the market."

Another sage reflection comes from William Kendall, famed for his spectacular exits, selling trendy soup-maker Covent Garden Soup for £20m in 1997 and upmarket chocolate company Green & Blacks for £25m in 2005.

For years, he was seen as an example to follow but he now describes exit-focused thinking as a "British disease" where people are in awe of someone selling up for millions but think nothing of the fact that they may have been employing 500 people, supporting entire local communities and investing in value through their activities across all stakeholders.

He told *The Daily Telegraph:*

"I regret selling Green & Blacks to Cadbury. It was a mistake, a great shame. I can say that now that Cadbury has pretty much disappeared, bought out by Kraft and now Mondalez. I wish I'd kept hold of it."

Kendall is adamant that entrepreneurs are under huge pressure to sell their businesses, simply because this is seen as the ultimate measure of success. This fallacy is borne out by the promotion of the agenda whereby the value of the entire business that someone has created is simply reduced to that of a brand. This is a wasteful and shameful reduction of what true greatness in business is.

Purposeful business leaders recognise that there is something much more important. They have found that one of the most sought-after skill-sets in today's complicated world is, quite simply, the ability to focus on what is most important and make whatever is desired happen. This is clarity of purpose.

This very simple statement is easier said than done, particularly when it involves the complexity of modern organisations, stakeholders and the myriad of influences that often can make it difficult for people and organisations to find such clarity.

Much of our experience is in the crossover between charitable, government and private-sector activities, but the methodologies and key factors to succeed in creating such focus transcend sectors and are applicable in all fields.

A journey into purpose activation

Each of us has a different story to tell; we create our own journey, based on where we were born, our family background and influences, early memories, life experiences, our loves and the sum of our years. All these go into making us what we are. It is why we are all individuals, unique in our own way and with a particular outlook on life and an approach to furthering our journey and supporting those we care for in theirs.

Where does a sense of purpose fit into this? When did the chief executives we have interviewed decide that they wanted to do things differently? What brought them to that point? What influences came to bear?

Later, we will look at how they activated those initial impulses to build successful purpose-led businesses. First, it is important to understand their motivations and the stories behind why they do things the way they do. We do so with one main purpose: to illustrate how a pathway to purpose can be adopted by anyone wanting to enhance their own life view.

It is only honest and open to declare our own journeys that have brought us to invest time and energy in exploring the purpose agenda.

 MEET JOHN

John grew up in a small English market town, where his large extended family engendered a strong sense of belonging. His family's businesses employed local people and he developed content in this microcosm, underpinned by a strong moral compass, based on regular church attendance, family values and a traditional work ethic.

After school, he worked briefly in retail banking before training as a British Army officer at the Royal Military Academy Sandhurst. He regards his commissioning as the most valuable experience of his life, progressing to serve for a decade as an infantry officer. "I benefitted from being absolutely purpose-driven, in an environment that continually invests in and tests that sense of purpose. It became the benchmark against which I can now clearly define whether my purpose is as strong as it should be."

After leaving the army 24 years ago, John learned his most valuable lessons about the power of purpose, declining the opportunity of a lucrative City career to chart a course focused on wider life decisions and interests. Beginning at a modest university-based medical research charity in Liverpool, he progressed via a local government role to oversee some of the Prince of Wales's personal charitable interests at Business in the Community, a leading proponent of the corporate social responsibility agenda.

There, he spent more than a decade working on social and environmental initiatives ranging from helping disadvantaged young people to encouraging responsible business leadership and promoting the rural agenda, inter-faith activity and sustainably built environments. "I found that when clarity of purpose prevailed within me, with alignment between why I wanted to do things and the "what" of the organisation I worked for, I was happier, more successful and had greater impact on the objectives in hand. I worked with like-minded people, had greater opportunities, found it easier to communicate to others and delivered much more substantial results."

John believes his Sandhurst training and the subsequent 10 years of operational experience around the world instilled clear strategic thinking, tactical application and an inherent desire to ensure that plans and people have the maximum opportunity to succeed. It also provided powerful experiences in areas of conflict, as well as the singular sense of purpose enjoyed by military units with strong common bonds.

His subsequent experiences were even more significant in shaping his thinking and purpose. In his 17 years working for the Prince of Wales, in various roles, both in the UK and on overseas assignments, launching programmes across 20 countries, his activities ranged from supporting the UK fishing industry to inspiring responsible business leadership, from flood relief in Pakistan to building communities via harmonious planning and architecture. He witnessed at close quarters how Prince Charles' sense of purpose led him to have a profound effect on many issues of concern, not least by creating the sense of greater collective purpose to attract other leaders.

Learning from the Prince's ability to convene, encourage, inspire and deliver has since seen John work with other senior business, government and charity-sector leaders. He has absorbed and integrated the lessons he has learnt from their highly varied approaches: "It has brought me into contact with all types of remarkable people – modest people who have created initiatives to lift local communities without achieving great recognition as well as more famous national campaigners who have led significant shifts in society overall."

 ## MEET ANDREW

Andrew, meanwhile, grew up as the son of a Baptist minister, moving from a tough environment near the Ford motor factory in Dagenham to a new council estate in Bootle, Merseyside and then to the edge of another local authority council estate on the edge of Cambridge.

At the heart of all three environments were close-knit local communities where the actions of unpaid leaders had a major effect on people's lives. He quickly observed how his father's status in his communities created a set of ethical expectations, not only of a minister of religion and his wife, who each had felt a clear calling to serve, but also in their offspring who actively had not made such a choice.

In eventually deciding to share his family's core beliefs, he was heavily influenced by his father, who developed a ministry among the dying and the bereaved. Working as free church chaplain in Cambridge's vast Addenbrooke's Hospital and later at a cancer hospice in Milton Keynes, he was on call at all hours of the day and night to provide solace and guidance for people in the most difficult times of their lives.

Andrew was struck by his father's gentle but insightful approach and also by the strong ethos among hospice staff and volunteers to provide patients with the best environments possible in their last days on earth.

Influenced also by his late grandfather, a former journalist at the *Daily Herald* newspaper, Andrew pursued journalism with a passion, working on magazines at school, setting up one at his church and editing the student newspaper at university. He then trained as a journalist and has been one ever since, working first for local papers in Oxford and then for *The Daily Telegraph* and *The Sunday Telegraph* in London and New York.

His work at a formative age included spending time with people bereaved by accidents and crime and he endeavoured to treat them with the compassion that he saw in his father. Then he became industrial correspondent, covering the motor industry, which led him into business journalism, within which his preferred field became interviewing chief executives and other prominent business people.

"In my daily work, I became fascinated by what makes CEOs tick and my first book, based on interviews with the leaders of two-thirds of the companies in the FTSE100 index, was really about understanding how they led the biggest firms in Britain. But, in doing that, I found those leaders with a purpose-led passion for what they were doing by far the most interesting. For me, the "why" then became all-important."

Your own experience

These are our experiences, but you will have your own, just as relevant in shaping an understanding of your own purpose and proposition and those of your businesses.

In reading this book, you have taken a decision either to learn more about purpose for yourself or your organisation, or you are already driving purpose but could do with some additional help on how to activate it more successfully.

Why you want to do this is another matter. Only you can determine why you truly do things. Only you can look deep into yourself and understand the influences that might range from childhood experiences to pressures of making ends meet in today's fast-driven consumer society. You are already motivated to make change happen in yourself and the world and this must mean that you have a vision around aspiring to improving something.

Your vision

Your vision is significant because becoming purposeful requires a sense of what you are aspiring towards, your desire for legacy in the change that purpose can bring and, a conviction about where you want your organisation to be positioned.

Such vision can be concerned with anything from sharing knowledge to building a more sustainable business, creating new technology to improve our existence or disrupting a specific sector.

But to achieve such goals, visions need to be capable of being embraced by others. That is where purpose has to become shared, or otherwise it simply cannot be achieved.

As Sir Tim Smit says:

> *"People bought into the vision of the Eden Project, and you do need to have a vision. I think a great company, a great charity, a great individual will sell a picture that, if you like good pictures, is of a stage on which the people they are addressing can imagine themselves standing. They will also get enough from the person talking to them to realise that, while they have the right amount of vanity to lead it, they are not so vain and weird that they're going to steal all the accolades and there's going to be enough space on that stage for everyone.*
>
> *"No one wants to work on a project with someone who says: "It's mine, mine, mine'. Like a vampire squid!"*

It is clear to anyone visiting Sir Tim's Eden or other projects that success has been achieved by a mission shared, not a mission just singularly owned.

The next step requires you to start to put yourself into the wider context. For an individual it will be your circumstances. For a business or organisation it will be your market.

However one is motivated around one's own purpose, what can sometimes happen is that when we then think clearly about what we believe our purpose is, we can run the risk of not being able to follow a course of action to make it part of our everyday life because other things get in the way.

We might conclude that we don't know how, or we lack the resources, money or skills required to follow the next steps beyond the stages that have got you so far. However, as you refine your sense of purpose, you will find empowerment in a new way.

History demonstrates that, when we get clarity of purpose, we then find the means of achieving it. It is how we have learned to fly, explored the moon, built extraordinary buildings and undertaken medical break-throughs. Clarity of purpose has been behind them all.

To feel a purpose and then feel unable to act, therefore, is contrary to all that we as a human race have undertaken to do over a millennium. Progress, moving forwards and creating change in the world to the benefit of others around us not only supports what we hope to affect individually but actually benefits ourselves in terms of our personal development and wellbeing.

Through such clear thinking, purpose and ideas, we can discover new skills, hidden depths of resolve and resilience, talents for things we hadn't been aware of and opportunities for our creativity to soar. We can culti-vate both the courage of our convictions and the inner satisfaction of knowing that, due to our own efforts, we are leaving the world a better place than it was.

Purpose into reality

There is nothing simple at all in turning your purpose into a behavioural reality. That is why we have chosen to share what many organisations and leaders ask us to assist them with. The fact is that sometimes clarity of purpose doesn't immediately emerge in organisations or in individuals naturally and yet many now seek it.

Given its significance, you must give it the best chance of being found. In our experience, the route prescribed in the following chapters, proven across many different assignments, affords you the best chance to create your own clarity of purpose and make that purpose happen.

That process in itself should make you feel purposeful. We all should recognise that, in creating our purposeful thinking and behaviours, we will start to set ourselves aside from the crowd. This makes us feel special, driven and thereby in ourselves elevated above those who lack such purpose. This is a natural adoption of a personal sense of status.

Robin Wight, without doubt the most colourful of advertising men and founder of public relations and marketing group Engine, says:

"We adopt status behaviour because that's the way we're wired up biologically."

We may find different ways of expressing it. Our wiring requires us to find a way to signal our genetic fitness. That is what status at the biological level is. Now for this generation it might be shoes or sneakers. It may be that we can make them more sustainable rainforest shoes. The ways in which status expresses itself will change, but it may not always be conspicuous consumption. It could be conspicuous non-consumption.

Finding your purpose

Some people will find purpose in other things, but for purpose in business you need to find it in yourself first. When we conducted our CEO interviews, we were struck by the frequency with which purpose-driven leaders cited a moment that filled them with deep conviction that they wanted to behave and operate differently.

For Business in the Community vice-president and former long-term chief executive Dame Julia Cleverdon, it was her incredulity at the leadership of British Leyland's Swindon body and assembly plant where she started her career in 1972.

"It was an absolutely scarring experience, because the front line of those working in the pressed steel shops and assembly and tool rooms absolutely minded and cared about what the company did and whether it created anything that anyone wanted to buy.

"But nobody in management appeared to be of the view that it mattered that workers should have information or that anyone

should bother to consult them or even that there might be people there that might know how to do things better. For me, that drove into beliefs that I still hold 44 years on.

"If you don't ensure that your people are engaged, involved and committed in the purpose of your business, how can you expect people to give their life's work, energy, time and commitment to it?"

Dame Julia suggested that the company took 20 body assembly workers to see their finished cars at the Birmingham Motor Show because they had never seen them. She was astonished at the management's response.

"I was taken aside and told that they had never heard of such a fatuous idea. The human resources director said: 'How on earth does it matter to them? You must realise that the world will never be changed and there is no point you trying to strive and urge that it should. These people don't mind what they're doing, it's just money to them.'

"That so entered my soul at that point that I have always believed that business has a noble purpose and that creating goods, services, income and jobs are immensely important and that people want to be proud of what they're trying to create in their organisations. That went on to be a theme throughout my life."

Brompton Bicycle managing director Will Butler-Adams, meanwhile, says he experienced his "values eureka moment" aged 19 when he nearly died on a trek through the Amazon where he got lost and wandered aimlessly for days. Convinced he was going to die there, he wrote his final words to his parents:

"When you think you're about to die, you reflect on things and know whether they are right or wrong. I decided there and then to be fair and reasonable in all I do. At the end of the day, you know what's right and wrong."

Later, he was attacked by a Bushmaster snake, killed it and ate it.

"It took about 10 days to get out and I had a lot of time to reflect. I wrote in my diary the things that mattered to me and

when I looked at life I realised that the most valuable things were the simplest, with my dearest friends."

Butler-Adams ran a chemical plant for ICI and moved to DuPont, but his life and career changed after he met the inventor's great friend, and chairman of Brompton Bicycles, Tim Guinness, on a bus in 2001. He joined the firm in 2002 and led a buyout in 2008. Now Brompton makes more than 45,000 folding bicycles a year and is Britain's largest bike manufacturer.

Brompton's stated purpose is: "Changing the way people live in cities." But Butler-Adams says:

> *"That's our purpose and it's very clear. But I didn't have that purpose when I started. The purpose came because I used the product and met people. In no way did we ever sit down and ask what was our purpose. It's defined by the business. It's not defined by us. It's an organic thing and it has developed over time."*

For Allirajah Subraskaran, founder of telecoms firm Lyca Mobile, the company's sense of purpose is closely linked to his own history, arriving in Europe at the age of eight from war-torn Sri Lanka. His family started running a corner shop in Paris where pre-paid international phone cards for immigrants to call home were one of the best-selling products sold.

When the distributor of the cards moved on to something else, he took up the distribution rights, later going a stage further with his London-headquartered business, which now buys telecoms capacity from larger telecoms groups and sells call packages on SIM cards.

The group now spans 20 countries, but Subraskaran says the focus of the company has stayed closely in line with the way the business developed:

> *"It's all about family and belonging for us. That's how we started, that's what we're about. We have 8,000 staff and we encourage people to bring their families to work for us. We see the company as one big family. It's about connecting, it's about being in touch and being real. That defines how we behave and everything we do."*

John Fallon at Pearson grew up in an educational background in the north of Manchester, as his father was a primary school head teacher. His grandfather was born in a poor house and grew up in an orphanage, learning how to become a tailor and educating his children. His mother left school at 15 as the eldest of 7 children and never had the benefit of an education that her husband or children had.

Fallon had no intention of entering business but now finds himself leading an education group employing 35,000 people. And his mother's experience has left him, as a father of daughters, acutely aware of the transforming power that education holds.

> *"I do think that actually working in a profit-making organisation you can play every bit as important a role in changing and shaping the world for better as you can in any other job."*

Driven by personal experience

Searing personal experience is a common factor behind purpose-driven business leaders. It has given many the energy and fervour not only to create businesses and generate value but to do so with a wider sense of purpose and mission.

Iqbal Wahhab

For Iqbal Wahhab, the restaurateur who created London's Cinnamon Club and Roast eateries, it was the realisation that two of his friends from a gang on a tough Battersea council estate ended up in prison, one committed suicide and another was killed.

> *"The rest have, at best, led unremarkable lives. They were all as smart as I was, some more so, which is why I have used whatever successes I have achieved to help open up opportunities for all.*
>
> *"I'm a self-made businessman, fully conscious of the fact that I could still be living in a ramshackle village in Bangladesh if my parents had not had the good fortune to make it to Britain. Had I not had a lucky break, I could have been like the other kids at my south London school who got into crime*

and drug addiction and ended up either in prison or dying at a tragically young age.

"As my business has developed over the years, I've always been conscious of not just where I can go next, but also of where I have come from –and who's still there."

Wahhab and John first collaborated some 10 years ago when John was creating the Mosaic mentoring network, one of the Prince of Wales's charities, with a mission to promote positive thinking through mentoring projects with young muslims.

John believed successful muslim leaders, with stories like Wahhab's, would be concerned enough to support interventions to address isolation in a younger generation. Wahhab answered the call and led a visit of business leaders to London's Wormwood Scrubs prison and was staggered to learn that about two-thirds of its young offenders ended up being imprisoned again soon after their release.

He found huge empty spaces in the prison that had once housed bakeries and a butchery but were now redundant because the prison bought in pre-prepared meals. He asked an inmate who was cooking meals for 200 prisoners what he intended to do on his release, only to find that he had no idea.

Wahhab told the prison governor that Britain's food industry was experiencing major skills shortages in butchery and bakery and that his own restaurant was being impeded by a difficulty in recruiting chefs. His words fell on deaf ears but he engaged more successfully with governors at Brixton and Isis Young Offenders Institute.

Wahhab's experiences since have left him with a strong belief that socially minded businesses are better placed than public bodies to be able to bring sustainable solutions to society's problems.

Roast began taking inmates on day release from The Clink, Brixton's on-site restaurant, some of whom have found jobs as a result. As word spread of this work, Roast received letters from people saying they had read of its prison work and would come to the restaurant as a result, a response that Wahhab views as a game-changer.

"It lifted my activities in these kinds of spaces away from being extracurricular, something I did while the business

carried on running its operation. It became a core activity, not one assigned to, at best, corporate social responsibility and, at worst, charity. The unintended but welcome surprise was that it was now proven to be good for business."

Annabel Karmel

Such formative experiences come in all shape and manner and with Annabel Karmel, the renowned children's food entrepreneur, her eponymous business and strong sense of purpose were borne out of personal tragedy.

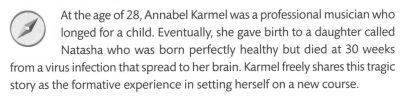 At the age of 28, Annabel Karmel was a professional musician who longed for a child. Eventually, she gave birth to a daughter called Natasha who was born perfectly healthy but died at 30 weeks from a virus infection that spread to her brain. Karmel freely shares this tragic story as the formative experience in setting herself on a new course.

"My whole life fell apart at that moment. It makes you think why you're doing what you're doing and for me playing music became something too superficial. I questioned why she was born and why this had happened to me. It's a life-changer losing a child and I knew then that I wanted to do something to help children's lives, to kind of make some meaning come from her death and to give something back. I didn't know at the time what it would be."

Karmel had another child within one year of Natasha's death, although it didn't quite go to plan as her obstetrician advised her to stay home when she rang to say she was in labour. She ended up giving birth on the staircase, her baby delivered into the arms of her husband. Not only was Nicholas's arrival somewhat dramatic, her new son had trouble eating and sleeping. Blessed with an incredibly fussy eater and feeling vulnerable having lost her first child, she combined a few things that he would eat with foods that he wouldn't, inventing recipes such as her recipe for chicken and apple balls.

She started a playgroup and discovered from other mothers that they had similar problems. She started printing out recipes for them and each week they would ask for more recipes, which led to a book called *The Complete Baby and Toddler Meal Planner*, which was endorsed by Great Ormond Street Hospital, where Natasha had died.

It became the UK's second best-selling hardback non-fiction book. Karmel has since published 42 books in 29 languages on feeding babies, toddlers and families, eating in pregnancy, cooking with children, and Mumpreneur – a practical guide on how to be a mother and a successful business woman. She has also filmed television series and launched a successful range of food products for toddlers and babies in the UK and abroad, which has turned into a £10m-a-year food business.

> *"I thought it would be a great legacy for Natasha. I never thought it would be a career. It helped me come to terms with her death. It's my driving force. I think that what you do for others will live on, while what you do for yourself will die with you. But it's not all about charity and doing good. It's also about people who have a reason to be in their business, which is also a profitable business.*

> *"There are so many pitfalls in business. It's not always great and you have days when you think 'Why am I doing this?' The 'why' keeps you going through the hard times."*

Chuck Runyon

Chuck Runyon, chief executive of Anytime Fitness, the American business that has become the world's biggest franchises gym operator with 3,500 sites in 29 countries, comes across many stories of high personal effort and achievement by the chain's members.

Indeed, he has published a book called *Bleed Purpose* to recognise the 3,000 Anytime Fitness gym members, staff and franchisees who have had the company's logo tattooed on their bodies.

> *"We're a family of healthy lifestyle enthusiasts who believe so fervently in what we're doing that we're willing to bleed purple literally. Over the years, thousands have chosen to have our logo emblazoned on different parts of their bodies. How many other franchisees feel that strongly about their brand? We have our own tattoo room at our headquarters and we had five of them at our last annual conference."*

While we have talked already about people's innate need to belong to something, tattooing one's employer's name on one-self is an extreme step. Runyon sees it as reflecting his company's purpose of helping people make the best of themselves. The company's core values are people, purpose, profits and play.

> *"Although it does show a gratitude to the brand, it's really about their self-expression and the progress of their journey they've been on, the results they've achieved or the role they've played in helping someone achieve a new definition of themselves. The reason is always very personal, very profound and unique. We're happy to be a small part of it.*

> *"I've heard hundreds of stories of why people do it and it is never about our treadmills or our being open 24 hours a day. It's always about the self-respect that someone now has, based on what they've been able to accomplish."*

Driven by beliefs

Another group of purpose-driven business leaders can be categorised as those who have closely held personal beliefs. Whether religious, humanist or simply based on love, care and respect for humanity, such convictions foment passion for doing business differently.

Ryan Gellert

One of the best-known examples is Patagonia, the outdoor clothing brand set up in 1973 by Yvon Chouinard, a Canadian with a business making metal pitons for rock climbing.

Patagonia was founded with a triple mission to "build the best products, do no unnecessary harm and to use business to inspire solutions to the environmental crisis".

The company is a founding member of a not-for-profit group called One Per Cent for the Planet, to which it donates 1% of annual gross revenues (about $6m a year) to charities working on sustainability issues.

Ryan Gellert, Patagonia's general manager for Europe, says the company's mission is inseparable from the Patagonia brand and has led it to take seemingly uncommercial action, such as taking out a full-page advert in *The New York Times* advising consumers "don't buy this jacket" on Black Friday, America's busiest shopping day of the year, in 2011.

It also runs a "Worn Wear" initiative, promising to repair old clothing and has ethical policies on the materials it uses in its products.

> *"What's always very interesting is when people hear the word Patagonia. What do they think first? Do they think 'great technical products' or do they think about a company with a unique set of mission and values? Sometimes it's one, sometimes the other, sometimes both. We're always proudest when it's both but we're very happy to have relationships with people who come to the company through either channel."*

Pat Gelsinger

For Pat Gelsinger, meanwhile, the purpose and values of VMware, the $32bn company he leads, are heavily tied up with his own personal religious beliefs. A committed Christian who nearly went into the church rather than technology, he gives away more than 40% of his salary, prays and sings hymns on journeys from his Californian office to the airport and resolved early in life never to read his daily business newspaper until he had read the Bible first.

Gelsinger grew up on a farm in Pennsylvania. His father was 1 of 9 children, while his mother was from a family of 11 and he skipped his last year of high school at the age of 17 to take up a scholarship to study electronics at Lincoln Technical Institute in his home state.

Gelsinger's faith clearly drives him. He led a weekly home bible study for 16 years and served as a Sunday school teacher, while his philanthropy supports medical relief, church planting organisations, educational work and an orphanage that he and his wife Linda helped build in Nairobi. He's written a book called *Balancing Your Family, Faith and Work*.

> *"There were a couple of moments of clarity of purpose for me. I became a Christian at the age of 18. It was a radical shift in my thinking and world view. I even thought of becoming a full-time minister but I became convinced that the workplace is my ministry and that the purpose we serve as leaders is a much bigger purpose."*

Leading a major quoted company with 18,000 employees with a clear sense of purpose is a world apart from doing so at a start-up. Yet Gelsinger is clear where the dividing line falls.

> *"Obviously I have to make the business successful. If the business is not successful, I need to be replaced. But if the business is successful, how do you define success? Clearly, there are financial metrics associated with the business but I am equally concerned about the people in my business, their careers and families and the communities that our business is part of.*

> *VMware's core values spell EPICC: execution, passion, integrity, customers and community.*

> *"We set up how we operate far above the legal requirement and independent of making the best revenue decisions. We want to make our customers successful. That's embedded in our culture and we're also deeply committed to the communities we serve. So I've seen this harmony of my own personal values with that of this company."*

Purpose as a turnaround methodology

Gelsinger and VMware demonstrate that clarity of purpose is not restricted to entrepreneurs and start-ups. By virtue of the numbers involved alone, it can actually be much more powerful when applied to existing companies that are much larger.

Indeed, clarity of purpose is an essential tool when attempting to turn around an organisation when it has lost its way, been outmanoeuvred by rivals or it has to adopt to changing market conditions. We'll discuss the latter in the next chapter, but first let's look at two companies where framing a clear sense of purpose has transformed underlying business.

Brad Smith

Intuit is a £29bn market capitalisation American company founded in California in 1983 by two entrepreneurs who saw that personal computers would lead to a demand for a computerised replacement for paper-and-pencil personal accounting.

It grew, attracting a takeover by Microsoft, which was blocked by anti-trust regulators, and subsequently had to fight off a competitive thrust by the Seattle-based company and others.

Led by chief executive Brad Smith since 2008, it has revenues of $4.2bn, a $29bn stock market capitalisation and a 92% share of the US small business accounting software market, with five million small business customers worldwide.

It moves 40% of tax returns in the USA, and helps small businesses and accounting firms comply with changing regulatory requirements. In recent times, it has moved its accounting to cloud computing.

Prior to Smith's appointment, Intuit was widely regarded as having lost its way, withdrawing from 18 international markets.

 Smith, who grew up in a working class family in West Virginia, has built on the company's original mission of improving people's financial lives. Indeed, the kitchen table on which Intuit's mission statement was written 34 years ago is now on show in the head office cafeteria.

> *"We have eight core values now. The first two are foundational and haven't changed since 1983: integrity without compromise and caring and giving back. The next six are: be bold, be passionate, be decisive, learn fast, win together and deliver awesome."*

The focus seems to be working as Intuit has been in *Fortune Magazine's* Top 100 Best Places to Work list for 15 consecutive years, something that Cisco Systems is the only other American technology company to achieve.

Smith also says that Intuit's voluntary staff attrition rate is 10%, compared to an average of 14% at other Silicon Valley firms.

> *"Millennials make up 49% of our workforce, and what we've learned is that they care more about why you exist as a company than what you actually make. So being environmentally conscious and socially oriented in terms of*

leaving the world better and interacting with other people, has been very important in creating the environment that has been conducive to getting them to come in and stay."

Graham Kerr

At South32, chief executive Graham Kerr has put values at the heart of the task of creating a company from scratch after being appointed in 2015 to lead the coal, nickel, manganese ore and aluminium business that has spun out of mining giant BHP Billiton.

"There were certain BHP core behaviours we wanted, but as a different company that had to be smaller, more agile and leaner we had to have a different set of values. The lead team described the kind of company we wanted and from there we gave it to some of our high-potential young employees to go out and work with each of the operations and talk about they wanted.

"They came back with the four values of caring, trust, togetherness and high performance and they were accepted by the leadership team and became the values of South32."

Kerr believes that it is critically important for South32 to have strong values as it starts its existence but adds that the reason for defining the new company's purpose runs deeper than that.

"We believe that if mining is done sustainably it can change people's lives forever. I've seen mining make a great difference to people's lives when I worked at a diamond mine in Canada's North West territories of Canada. It created an enormous amount of employment and educational opportunities and wealth and it did so in one of the world's most pristine environments and generated a good return for shareholders. It showed that you can get the balance right."

He is realistic enough to recognise that choosing a new company's values has to be a much more deep-rooted effort than simply picking its name.

"We've been running cultural change for about 18 months, but cultural change takes at least 3 or 4 years to bed

into your business. We're different from BHP Billiton in many ways. The culture is different from the top down in our board, our leadership team, how we position ourselves and how we try to operate,

"We're much more open. The board mixes in the cafeteria with employees and our chairman plays table tennis with them. That didn't happen at BHP Billiton. We're trying to build a much more open environment where people feel that their voice can be heard. But there's a fair way to go yet."

Chapter summary

The above illustrate clearly some of the personal and business drivers that vary from case to case but have, effectively, brought people to the same purpose path.

If you are reading this and find it hard to know how to gain such clarity, be assured, in many cases such understanding only comes much further down the journey than at the start point.

Many of those we know wouldn't necessarily have appreciated at the time that they were headed in that direction. However, we believe, and our experiences now bear out, the fact that such a journey can be planned rather than simply emerge over time. Indeed, the forces ranged against conventional business now demand such proactive development.

With this in mind, you now need to consider your ability to find purpose in business.

- **What do you want from business?** This is where you have to be clear that your personal sense of purpose, desires and interests are deliverable through a business and working for business. If you cannot see how this works for you, then you may be better placed in the public or charitable sectors.

- **What does the business want from you?** Do the culture, hours, values, colleagues and type of work match with your own? If there's a mismatch here, you will be unlikely to find such purpose satisfaction in this particular organisation.

- **What does the world want from the business?** Can the business meet the need and are you happy with that demand? If you aren't happy producing a particular product, or offering a service, but the world demands it, you will become discontented.

In attempting to address these three points, ask yourself the questions below. Through these and such reflection you should be able to clarify that your purpose can be achieved through business.

1. **What do you need in terms of comforts?** Answer in terms of salary level, but also levels of risk, working conditions and other practical aspects that you have as your minimum comfort level. Identify what you really need, rather than just assuming you need what everyone else may consider the norm.

2. **What would you like to feel you achieve?** Assess the things within your work that you would feel proud of saying to others, such as friends and family. These factors will shape your thinking around how your actual activity in business is aligned to what you feel motivated by.

3. **What do you feel you can most contribute?** Think about the skills and attributes you offer. These can be formal, such as qualified skills, or characteristics such as your drive and enthusiasm. The critical thing is whether they will be appreciated by the business. This will help you see yourself in a work environment with like-minded people.

4. **What type of culture does the business expect you to be a part of?** Major issues have arisen in recent years where certain corporate cultures have been oppressive, too demanding in terms of hours, discriminatory and other negative attitudes. Not all people are even happy in positive cultures where certain group activity or behaviour is the norm. Consider carefully what this means for you.

5. **What is the business' expectation on your role?** Does the level of responsibility match your interest or the future prospects of progress, recognition or flexibility you have or can aspire to in order to afford you the opportunity to make a purposeful contribution?

6. **Does your business have an ambition that aligns with your own?** To consider the prospects of both yourself and the business will offer you the foresight to see how you both can grow through the

combination of your efforts and that of the wider team. Consider if these aspirations are compatible.

You should now have a clearer understanding of what the world is likely to expect from the business – and, by default, yourself.

For example, if the world is demanding your business competes on price rather than quality and it leads the business to incentivise internal behaviour in a way that you think compromises the values, the purpose and yourself, it will not work.

Therefore, understanding and appreciating where there is a mismatch between your clear sense of purpose and how the business operates in the world is fundamental to addressing this question.

 If you can answer to your satisfaction the three questions in the diagram below, then the sweet spot in this regard is where you will find yourself.

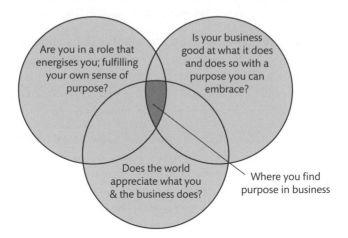

Are you in a role that energises you; fulfilling your own sense of purpose?

Is your business good at what it does and does so with a purpose you can embrace?

Does the world appreciate what you & the business does?

Where you find purpose in business

Having found your purpose in business

This chapter has combined your appreciation of your personal sense of purpose and how it can be amplified and applied through business.

A very useful and universally accepted model is illustrated below.

It very simply expresses the harmony between what you care about, what you are good at, what your business does and what the world needs.

As shown, such purpose when discovered mobilises your sense of passion, creates a mission focus, allows you to become valued as a professional and in turn sees the world value your business. This is the overarching personal ambition for purpose-driven individuals.

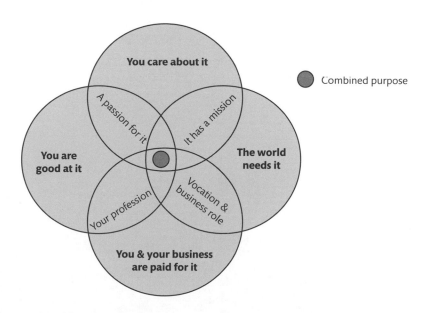

Chapter 3

Define your world

Introduction

It was over ten years ago that, John (now Lord) Browne, then chief executive of BP, spoke at the British Museum on the responsibility of business and, in particular, considered the significance of being alert to the world. He used museum exhibits from ancient Venice, one of his personal passions, to tell the story of business in the archipelago, with lessons on long-term sustainability and why once the merchants of Venice lost their sense of purpose in the world they lost their regional dominance of trade.

He cited the scene in Shakespeare's *The Merchant of Venice* where one businessman asks another, "What news on the Rialto?" summarising what was up, down and happening in the world generally.

Browne went on to explain that, when they stopped asking the questions, they stopped being ahead of the game.

In this phrase, the question being asked seems simple but now must be asked of you today. It means a purpose-driven leader needs to be interested in society and in what's happening in new learning, technology advances and in progress generally. If you stop or never ask the questions, you will fail to understand the world you are trying to change.

The reason for this is that the way we perceive ourselves and our business relates greatly to how the rest of the world influences our behaviours, values and beliefs. You can become a purposeful leader only by understanding the world you occupy and how it influences you. And that world incorporates wider society and its norms, the market and its influences, the social and family world you occupy and the world from which you gain intellectual stimulation.

Together, these make the world as we prescribe it for this purposeful journey and, yet, every one of us will occupy a world unique only to us.

This is, therefore, by default, a dynamic combination of cognition, perception, learning, emotion, attitudes and relationships that have played with us throughout our lives. As with our own personal journeys, these reflect the influences on how we assess our world from a business perspective.

The influences on us

These factors are all relevant in understanding the ways that we choose to manage our interactions with other people, other organisations, businesses, governments, places and things. We are influenced by issues as wide-ranging as prejudice, romantic attractions, persuasion, friendship, conformity, group memberships, our schooling and whether we live in urban or rural locations.

There is an interesting website called The Global Rich List (www.global-richlist.com) that allows people to measure their estimated wealth against that of every other human being on earth.

 Given one's starting position – growing up wherever you did is simply an accident of birth – and only what you do after that can really be down to you. In taking such a step forward and declaring yourself to the world in whatever way you wish, as a purpose-driven business leader, you need to understand your place in that world. Rightly or wrongly, so much is valued today by the perception of material wealth, which creates an accepted measure of influence, power and ability. So how wealthy do you think you are?

By our thinking, just about anyone who does this Global Rich List assessment and finds themselves in the top 10% of the world, which is likely to be nearly everyone reading this book, should have something of a responsibility to try and turn their personal purpose into a wider one that can affect the lives of all those who aren't so fortunate.

Having established a sense of place in the world, think again about your own journey and how it has been shaped. Consider how it would be perceived by someone observing you.

To do this, you need to take note of both your own place in the world around you and that of your business. Then the challenge is to understand how your business operates in its marketplace and how it could do so more effectively if it dovetailed more effectively with how society views the role of business and its responsibilities.

Changing the world

Leaders willingly take on this journey and some of the best ones have overcome significant challenges in confronting worlds that they know have to change.

Dame Inga Beale is a key example. The second child of an English father and Norwegian mother, she went into insurance aged 19 and worked for 31 years in the industry before being appointed the first female chief executive of the Lloyd's insurance market.

Dame Inga is the first female CEO in the market's 331-year history and needed talent as well as hard graft to get to the top. But she also prioritised her out-of-office lifestyle, playing competitive rugby for Wasps into her thirties and taking a year off to go cycling in Australia and back-packing through Asia.

She came out as bisexual in 2008 and married in 2013. Appointed at Lloyd's in 2013 to lead the still heavily male and pale traditional insurance market, she set an agenda based on her passion to modernise it.

Her actions included establishing an annual Diversity Festival in London to encourage racial, gender and sexual diversity. Lloyd's was an unlikely candidate to sponsor such an event, given its striking lack of diversity at the time. However, holding the event was an important indicator of the direction of the market and a valuable commitment to the movement.

> *"When I started out in my career, I didn't think I had a purpose at all and work was just a means to earn some money to go and do my sport. That's how I started and it wasn't really until I was challenged by an individual at Lloyd's to define my purpose for myself in life that I began to think about it. I had never thought about it or planned my life or career.*
>
> *"This got me thinking and I decided there was an aspect in me that actually says I want to make a difference to women in business. It goes back to the 1980s and the City of London where I felt like a lone female.*
>
> *"My desire to ensure that women can be successful in business has now broadened into a passion for wider diversity and inclusion that goes beyond gender. I want to tackle the tradition*

of the City and redress the balance between the people who have always done well there against those that have felt unwelcome."

This is Dame Inga's passion and she has set about it with great energy at Lloyd's. This drive has also been fused with a vision for the market based on an understanding of its history and role in protecting society through changing times. And it has also had to connect with apparent contradiction that the world she occupied is changing on the one hand, yet resistant to such change on the other.

"Since I've taken on the Lloyd's role, I've become much more philosophical about what insurance does. I've always known it has a really good social purpose but as I understood more about Lloyd's, I saw how it has been underwriting human progress over the centuries.

"What Lloyd's stands for is enabling the world to move ahead. Look at the example of cyber attacks. They're just everywhere. But here we are providing insurance and advising how to protect people's businesses because this new risk has come along. Fundamentally we underwrite human progress and we are alongside society as it goes through that."

At Unilever, meanwhile, Paul Polman's commitment to long-term sustainability has led him to make public statements on human rights, violence and discrimination against women, sustainable development and infrastructure, climate change and many other important subjects in our changing world. At Unilever, he says the brands that meet the highest standards for social and environmental impact are growing 40% faster than the rest of the company's products.

"What we've learned most is that for a brand to connect with people in today's highly transparent and interconnected world, it doesn't just need to meet an individual's goals but to provide solutions that help society thrive.

"This is what builds relationships between brands and consumers and ultimately drives high brand equity and sales. Doing this means developing brand content that doesn't just cut through the clutter but that inspires people to talk about the brand, share it, engage with it and help build it, which ultimately results in

positive movement for change. After all, the purpose of business is to serve – and not take away from – the communities and societies on which it relies for its very existence."

From the digital age to a purpose-led era

We say purpose is the biggest radical non-technological factor that will affect business this century. However, we also acknowledge that technology is the basis on which so much of the purpose that leaders rely upon is founded. The impact of the digital age is therefore highly significant, not least as a catalyst for the whole purpose-related movement.

In healthcare, Kieran Murphy, chief executive of General Electric's healthcare life sciences business, sees digitalisation of data linked to GE's stated purpose to "improve lives in the moments that matter" and the purpose of his division of the company to "create capacity and deliver productivity".

These purposes are linked to GE's five core beliefs:

- Customers determine our success.

- Stay lean to grow fast.

- Learn and adapt to win.

- Empower and inspire each other.

- Deliver results in an uncertain world.

 He believes the digital age is enabling social benefits, including the better use of electronic health records and genomics, including linking genetic predispositions to health outcomes and disease states.

"We're living in a world that's rapidly evolving because of new technology, particularly in digital, and we're excited about a more digital future in healthcare. We see the opportunity for cost reduction in healthcare being primarily linked to the ability to provide better analytics at patient and hospital systems level and for the whole pharmaceuticals industry.

"Technologies like 3D printing are going to completely change the world and machine learning and artificial intelligence are going to have a huge impact on the productivity of healthcare systems in the future.

"And if you think about the way our technologies are used for diagnosing disease or creating the opportunity for treatment, they make a huge difference to peoples' lives. Creating purpose statements has been a galvanising and unifying force for the business."

When you are assessing your world, it will, undoubtedly, include how technology can be applied to serve your purpose, how your markets may have been expanded through the world shrinking and even in a very practical way where you can get resources, collaborators and suppliers to move your business forward. The digital age and all it offers us is an amazing facilitator, with entire industries now well established that couldn't exist otherwise. However, such digital ability is simply "what" can be used, or "how" something is undertaken, which we contend is still not as powerful as "why" we do things.

The "digital age" will be surpassed by the "purposeful age".

This book isn't going to set out how powerful a tool it is for you but we do ask you to consider that everything that affects your ability to drive a purpose business has now become closer.

Cultural significance of the global age

One of the major points for consideration is the culture and society expectations within which you will be operating.

Multinational firms now operate in a manner where they are essentially borderless, with work being passed across continents, let alone countries. They and you (if this is in your world) will have to consider the cultural variability of different parts of the world and develop deeper cultural understanding.

We have actually advised on the differences between the West and Muslim countries where various cultural aspects can, at first appearance, seem to be obstacles.

If you are clear on your purpose, then initial obstacles can be seen as opportunities for innovation, new ways of working, products and services. What this demonstrates clearly is the distinction between what you do and why you do it.

Take one example: if you were a food company and had a range of products which, when taken to a new culture, were deemed unacceptable either for religious or cultural reasons, you have a stark choice. You either withdraw from that market or you put the product to one side, focus on your desire to feed people and create a new product that serves that purpose better.

That is a very simple example but it illustrates why understanding the world you are operating in will allow you to be more attuned to the application of clarity of purpose to overcome and succeed.

 Fast food giant, McDonald's has a global operating presence in more than 100 countries. Its headquarters is in the USA but global success has come about by basing and empowering people in each of these countries to make the right decisions in line with the company's stated purpose of going beyond what it sells to use its global and social reach to be a positive force for its customers, employees, communities and world.

This works because the menus are customised according to the cultural, religious and culinary tastes of each country. In doing so, the company's focus is on the purpose of the business, not its most famous USA-originating products such as the Big Mac.

Market influences and demands

We all have basic physical needs such as air, water, food, clothing, warmth and safety. But understanding your market is about the social needs for belonging, knowledge, self-expression and what we now see as the normal requirements of life.

In the marketplace in which you are going to operate, you need to understand the influences, quality, value, price, services and delivery. Will people pay extra for an "ethical" product? Such demands will shape your own view and, ultimately, the success in any given market, but they are also shaped by the cultural norms and expectations we alluded to earlier.

For example, everyone needs food and water to survive, but an American wants to have a Big Mac, French fries and a bottle of Cola. A British person might want fish and chips and a cup of tea with milk and sugar, while a Chinese person wants to have noodles or rice, fried vegetables and meat, and another altogether different cup of tea.

What this simply means is that you, like any other business person, must be close to the market (the world) you hope to service and provide for. This can include your suppliers, service delivery people and others who make valuable contributions to the market you are creating.

At online gifting marketplace Notonthehighstreet.com, the company attaches enormous importance to its partners – the 5,000 craft and artisan small businesses that create products marketed through its web platform.

The company has a programme called "In your shoes" whereby its 230 staff each spend two days a year working alongside a partner, helping make products, uploading them on the internet, helping with marketing or doing whatever the business needs.

Chief executive Simon Belsham says:

> *"Our people will do whatever a partner needs on those days. It's about working alongside the partners to help our people understand what it's like for them. It's a key part of how we engage our partners and it helps engage our staff too."*

Notonthehighstreet.com measures the engagement of its partners through a twice-yearly survey called "The partner voice". It focuses on how they are supported in their communities. One of the first questions is: How is Not On The High Street helping you grow your business?

The survey also asks what more the company can do to help them host "Make do and meet" events around the UK, that gather together groups of 100 to 150 partners to give them access to senior management and keep them updated on the company's direction.

The business also holds live webinars for partners and organises an internal social network.

> *"That community engagement is a way for our partners to feel a member and a part of something. It's an extraordinary embodiment of how technology can be used to drive*

engagement with the world around a company and it has a direct impact on Notonthehighstreet.com's workforce and business.

 "We measure purpose in a number of ways, including a twice-yearly survey of our staff. One of the things we ask is: Why do you work for Notonthehighstreet.com?'

"More than 90% of employees say the reason they work here is because of what we stand for, because of our purpose. As we bring in new people and evolve the business, how we help people understand that and induct then into that is a core part of what we do.

"I spend an hour with every employee that joins the business, talking about where it came from, its history, rationale and purpose and its strategy for the future. It's really important that they hear it from me or the founders. And it actually helps them do their jobs better. It helps them understand because our partners use our technology."

Strong purpose-driven businesses understand all these influences so that with their customers they aim to connect on the purpose – the why they do something – as much as, if not more than what they produce. They are effectively trying to turn conventional customers into "raving fans".

In their respective books *Creating Raving Fans* and *Re-imagine*, business gurus Ken Blanchard and Tom Peters both recognise this phenomenon as a key commercial driver. But they base their analyses on the fact that customers need to feel that the service they receive is personal in order to move them beyond merely being "satisfied" to become advocates.

For Ryan Gellert at Patagonia this connects with how the marketing of the US outdoor clothing retailer's products is effectively driven by how aficionados of the brand promote and advertise the company's core values and products. It's something that is reinforced by how deeply purpose is ingrained in its workforce.

"It doesn't take long walking around our headquarters, meeting the people and seeing how we're set up, to really understand that this is pretty key for us.

"We do a lot of training here and in the field. We have someone who travels the world giving philosophy classes and talking about the foundation of our principles. Although we have a team of people working very specifically in environmental and social initiatives globally, we keep that team really small because we want to make sure that our values and commitments are embedded across the organisation and teams, instead of having just one group that focuses full-time on them."

Opportunity from social trends

Being aware of the world will also allow you to build opportunity based around your purpose. One example is how UK supermarkets and farmers saw the emergence of consumers' concerns for the purity of their food.

Alongside rising disposable incomes, this has led to an expansion of locally sourced products and organic and natural foods, providing business opportunities for companies that saw this trend and were genuine about addressing it because of their core beliefs, as well as because it was another chance to sell value-added goods.

At Booth's Supermarkets, Edwin Booth says:

"Success and growth can be wrapped up in the word 'prosperity'. It's about value for more people and it doesn't have to be just about money. That's really important in this day and age. It's about an all-encompassing value."

 Increasing environmental awareness also has implications for other businesses, benefiting Brompton Bicycle's stated purpose to change the way that people live in cities:

Will Butler-Adams, MD of Brompton Bicycle, says:

"Initially, we couldn't have been as arrogant as to have that vision because we weren't exporting enough and we didn't have enough insight into what was happening on a global scale. But as we have been more aware of what's happening on a global scale, our purpose has grown stronger and our clarity has become clearer."

Butler-Adams believes other world developments have also benefited Brompton's model.

> *"Our business spread through word-of-mouth. And, as the internet and social media revolution arrived, word-of-mouth went global, which was very good for our business. But it also means we have to stick by what we believe. If we do something wrong, everybody gets to hear about it almost immediately."*

There are other trends, too, most notably a growing concern about the quality of life in some parts of Britain among those in society who are "just managing".

Edwin Booth believes that in these days of major hypermarkets, it is important for his smaller, more community-focused grocer to demonstrate its commitment to its localities. When a customer didn't appear at the company's store in Ilkley, West Yorkshire, for a couple of days in mid-2016, a checkout operator visited the woman's house to see if she was all right.

> *"It was an extraordinary thing to do but so meaningful in many ways. It turned out the customer was very poorly and we were able to help out and ensure that the various services were alerted.*

> *"Running a business for us is about being part of a community, however big or small. It's about being human. By exercising our family beliefs in the way we do business. We empathise with far more people than we would reach if we just had a structure that delivered boxes and products to the front end. And our employees derive massive satisfaction from the smile on someone's face when they go the extra mile to help them with something."*

Booth sees society's demand on business changing as recognition spreads, that simply posting growth in gross domestic product leaves many parts of an economy untouched.

> *"Efficiency can rail against humanity sometimes. We're all trying to create a wealthier society but wealth is about more people being engaged doing something economically useful and valuable to their peers and colleagues.*

"The developed world has a massive challenge at the moment and I think the West is going to almost hit the buffers in terms of finding means by which to simply sell more stuff to people."

The Roots of Responsible Business

This has a root going back to the early days of Business in the Community where the first founding members created the phrase "to have vibrant high streets, you need vibrant side streets", meaning that they understood the wider world they were trying to operate in, the levels of prosperity or otherwise being key to their prospects.

 Sir Mike Rake is chairman of BT Group and a former chairman of both Business in the Community and president of the Confederation of British Industry. He sees three waves of realisation that clarity of purpose is the key to successful businesses, each of which is directly related to world events.

The first, he says, followed the Brixton riots of 1981, with the evolution of Business in the Community and the Prince's Trust. Business, he recalls, couldn't just sit back and watch what was happening and decided that it had to do something to build community and society. That led to the entire CSR movement in the UK and created much improvement in business practices, including particular activities between businesses and local communities, as well as education, mentoring and looking after the underprivileged.

The second phase came when businesses realised that the agenda had to become broader, embracing the environment impact of the business and extending into sustainability.

Now, he believes there is a third stage, catalysed by the 2008 financial crisis, following which Western society has grown to distrust the political and business establishment. That third phase is the emergence of purpose as the definitive all-encompassing rationale for business.

Businesses that recognised these influences came together in 2011 under the banner of "A Blueprint for Better Business", a movement that began as a result of a number of UK business leaders approaching the Roman Catholic Archbishop of Westminster.

Sir Mike, chairman of the advisory committee for the Blueprint Trust, which supports the movement, says:

> *"What came out of this process was a conviction that business with real purpose is business that is sustainable and successful."*

The core of the blueprint model is a commitment to deliver value through an explicit purpose and the resulting quality of the human relationships nurtured internally and externally. It is a highly accessible but equally challenging model for both the business and leaders looking for such purpose and is proving highly popular.

The principles of the blueprint are freely available at their website.

Brands that resonate

Cilla Snowball, Group Chairman and chief executive of advertising and communications group AMV BBDO, agrees that brands have to be real to be relevant in today's world and that means resonating with what is happening in the world.

> *"We have a range of clients and perspectives, and we can see that brands with both a purpose and platform engage in a more effective way and achieve greater consistency, returns and loyalty from their customers and colleagues than brands that don't express a purpose.*
>
> *"We see where values really make a difference. It goes much deeper than communications and it's not all about millennials. Purpose has become a very important factor in the attraction and retention of talent. It has become a leadership imperative."*

Snowball sees brands responding to the world's changing attitudes to diversity and the importance of social inclusion across differences of gender, race, age and sexuality. She cites these examples:

- Unilever's initiative to take stereotypes out of its advertising.
- Procter & Gamble's work in India to encourage men and women to share domestic washing loads.

- Diageo's purpose-centred programme around the Rugby World Cup, featuring openly gay rugby star Gareth Thomas in a campaign for Guinness.

"There's some mould-breaking work going on. We hadn't done an LGBT campaign for Guinness before but this was a real story around purpose and inclusion. There's something very hard-nosed about purpose. It's about doing the right thing as well as about doing the best thing commercially.

"This is what the consumer now demands of brands in a world where they are more accountable than ever before, due to social media. But what's new is the sense of a collaborative, more shared purpose, rather than just a brand purpose."

Some of these challenges are even more acute outside the UK and, for some companies and executives, their "world" – not least because of their markets – is much larger than simply a domestic view.

A global perspective

Tej Kohli, an Indian billionaire and entrepreneur who seeks to make disruptive investments in the finance, digital media, medical science and renewable energy sectors, sees four major reasons why the world is changing for the worst.

"The first reason is globalisation, which has made the poor poorer and the rich richer. Globalisation in the end is a very positive thing but it has hurt some people in the short run. No business can be profitable without taking account of globalisation. But at the moment, globalisation is a major reason why we're going through such humongous changes.

"The second reason is demographics. You only have to look at Japan to see what is happening in Europe now with ageing populations and a lack of young enterprise.

"The third problem is automation, which is going to have a major effect once driverless cars come into being and more robots are used in other fields such as healthcare. A lot of people are going to be out of business and there's no obvious way of replacing all the jobs lost.

"Finally, there's $230 trillion of debt in the world. When you put all these things together in the next five years, it's a perfect storm. It's going to turn the world upside down and that process has only just begun."

That's the context in which Kohli sees the debate around purpose, yet his own stated purpose is highly ambitious. Within his aim of making business investments that make an impact for the betterment of society, Kohli is working to transform agricultural irrigation with plastic solar water pumps that cost-effectively can help meet the challenge of feeding India's growing populations.

He plans to loan thousands of pumps to farmers at rates that make their investment in high production capability worthwhile but also generate profits for his own businesses.

Second, he is committed to trying to eradicate corneal blindness by 2030, a sizeable goal since the condition currently accounts for 4.9 million of the world's blind.

Kohli's foundation is working to tackle the problem at a hospital in Hyderabad, India and through his own Tej Kohli Corneal Institute.

"We're aware of the need to counter these massive headwinds. Some of them scare us to death but we're going to try and do what we want to do anyway. How you tackle these issues will make you or break you."

While our interviews for this book brought forth many world views, Kohli's was one of the most comprehensive, and yet succinct, in laying out the global context for the future of society and business and the challenges and opportunities that exist within that.

Involvement in emerging markets

It's the sort of insight one can only really develop with operations in the field. Former Aviva chief executive Richard Harvey is another example of it, having taken a year off to work for charities in Africa before returning to a portfolio career in the UK, including a period chairing PZ Cussons, the soap manufacturer with major business in emerging markets. He says some knotty ethical issues cannot be avoided when major Western businesses are involved in emerging markets.

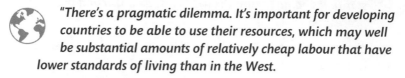 *"There's a pragmatic dilemma. It's important for developing countries to be able to use their resources, which may well be substantial amounts of relatively cheap labour that have lower standards of living than in the West.*

"You're not going to have a sustainable business if you try to pay everybody in a developing country what you would pay them to work in the UK. That doesn't work, so you'll always have that dilemma but I think the answers are in genuine practical things.

"At PZ Cussons, we insisted that the health and safety standards in those factories were the same as if they were in the UK because human life is just as precious wherever it is. We wouldn't pay people the same as it would be impractical to do so. But we tried to be fair in our working practices and broadly gave people the same kind of working rights they would have as a Westerner.

"Then it very quickly gets down to basic processes about what you're doing and how you're treating the environment where your factory is. What are you doing with your waste? Are you being sensible with what you're using for your power? And how are you cleaning up your waste water? It's about those kinds of nitty-gritty things."

A North American perspective

In America, footwear and apparel entrepreneur Jay Coen Gilbert, a cofounder of B Lab, the not-for-profit organisation behind the B Corp movement, seeking to change the standards to which private businesses are held, notes the current turbulence in American and world politics.

"What's happened here is not that different from what's happening in the UK with the Brexit vote or lots of other things going on around the world due to a populist anger that the system has failed them. I think we're now sitting in the same carriage as everyone else in that regard."

Coen Gilbert sees this as further stimulating the movement for greater accountability in business.

> *"My sense of purpose in what I hope to do with the one life I have got has always been pretty clear to me. But it wasn't part of some bigger movement; it was personal. At AND 1, Jay's basketball footwear and apparel business prior to B Lab, we wanted to run a business we would be proud of and that meant treating the people in it like partners, whether they were, the 200 people on our direct payroll or the 20,000 young women in the factories where our goods were made in and around Asia, and making sure that we were doing right by them.*

> *"We knew we were born into significant privilege and wanted to act in a way that was worthy of that. People might think that you make cool t-shirts and shoes but being cool is very different from being meaningful. We aspired to take a platform that was about being cool and, even though our customers didn't know or care, turn it into a platform from which we could be meaningful."*

The B Corp movement is now growing across the globe providing, alongside organisations such as Blueprint, better business collective opportunities to work with other businesses on a purposeful transformation.

A banking perspective

The global financial crisis and the continued fallout in consumer perceptions have had a particular impact on Britain's banks, with surveys regularly showing that banks have lost customers' trust and are poorly regarded.

 However, understanding this development has led to opportunities for banks innovative or flexible enough to respond to clearly stated changing customer preferences.

Craig Donaldson, chief executive of Metro Bank, the "challenger bank" set up by American banking executive Vernon Hill, grew up in a mining village in North East England before working for banks including Barclays, HBOS and Royal Bank of Scotland, where he was shaken by the impact of the banking meltdown of 2008.

> *"It was horrible for everybody, but yes it was horrible and I was not proud."*

When he was approached by Vernon Hill to help lead his new venture, Donaldson saw the opportunity to reinvent British banking by making it accessible to grassroots people (and took a major pay cut to join Metro).

"I'm a big believer in community. I saw that Vernon's Commerce Bank in the US was loved by customers, shareholders and staff and wondered how a bank could get all three right when most organisations struggle to get one of them right."

Donaldson was struck by Hill's passion for making customers into fans, something we have seen elsewhere.

"The model has to be focused on creating fans and the culture has to be fanatical about the model. I was engaged by this eccentric American. We're very different but his model was exactly what I wanted to do. He was so proud of what he had done in the US and didn't have to apologise for it. I thought that it would be nice to not have to apologise for being a banker in the UK."

Metro bank opens seven days a week, calls its branches stores and attracts customers with long opening hours, friendly, accessible policies and a flat structure. Its stated mission is to be the country's "premier financial conglomerate, empowering individual and business clients to realise their goals and reach their full potential". To do that, it commits to being a trusted financial partner, employer of choice, responsible bank and "an institution with a heart".

"We have a zealot-like focus on customers and when you combine that with genuinely good banking, you get something special.

"I wanted to do something to make my family proud. We wrote the vision and values of the organisation over some beers in a pub. I've got them hanging up at home on two beer mats. I've had them framed. We wanted to build something that people could believe in and get behind.

"The vision is where we're going and values are how we get there. We go through them with everybody who joins the business. I'm the first person to speak to everybody who joins and we go though the vision and values of the company because it's really important everyone understands what we are."

Incumbent banks also have a major opportunity to differentiate themselves through purpose. At TSB Bank, chief executive Paul Pester's background is as a consultant with McKinsey and banker at Virgin Money, Santander and Lloyds Banking Group.

"A sense of purpose has really crystallised at TSB, but it has been informed by what I've seen in previous roles. In setting up Virgin Money where I was the CEO, I worked directly for Richard Branson and I learned from him that why businesses exist is absolutely key.

"As TSB was created from 630 branches that Lloyds Banking Group had to sell, this meant purpose has been everything for us. On day one, we were trying to create a new bank but another bank had the same products, services, systems and capability. How can a bank compete with another when it is like that and one quarter of its size?"

Pester found the answer by talking to banking customers and looking at the history of TSB, whose brand was being revitalised to market the new bank.

"We talked to customers about why there was such a visceral hatred of banks in the UK following the banking crisis and what they wanted to see from banks. We found a very clear statement that consumers and society at large wanted to see banks get back to their original purpose, which is to help communities thrive and to help hard-working local people help themselves.

"At the same time we looked at the history of TSB which has a fantastic heritage going back to 1810 when it was set up by Henry Duncan, a Scottish vicar as the world's first self-supporting savings bank. He did that because labourers needed £100 to open a bank account and that was about what they earned a year.

"He set it up in the local church hall and used it as a way to help his parishioners out of poverty. So we were learning about this heritage at the same time as understanding that what customers really wanted was a bank that got back to the purpose of banks and so we decided that was exactly the way we would run this business.

"The reason we're here is to bring more competition to UK banking and ultimately make banking better for all UK consumers. We're doing that by bringing local banking back to Britain with a bank that's there to serve the local community of which it is part and nothing else. We have no investment banking, no derivatives trading and no overseas investments. We're crystal clear on that."

Purpose does not have to be soft and mushy. Indeed, Bel Lepe, cofounder of American video technology company Ooyala, sees it as something quite hard-edged. Ooyala's stated purpose is to be the leader in video monetisation in a way that helps its customers retain and grow their brands.

"Ultimately, we have that purpose and then we have values such as transparency and customer focus that support it. But we also have a core value around the notion of hustle and grit. This is a hard industry that we're in and you don't get anywhere without being scrappy. These are the centres of gravity that we look for in candidates and are core to defining what we are."

Chapter summary

Such clarity of purpose, allied to a genuine understanding of a business's place in the world that it serves, is the foundation stone for a successful business that delivers long-term sustainable growth and has the power to change society for the better. That's the challenge for purpose-driven leaders in all sectors of the economy.

The World and Sustainability Development Goals

We cannot talk about your place on the world without at least referencing The Sustainable Development Goals (SDGs), which replaced the Millennium development goals in 2015 and defined 17 global sustainable development priorities and aspirations for 2030. They were established to try and inspire global efforts around a common set of goals and targets with a worldwide call for action from governments, business and civil society organisations to end poverty and create a life of dignity and opportunity for all, within the environmental considerations of the planet.

Purposeful business can play a part

Business has a critical role to play in supporting the achievement of these goals. Regardless of size, a business and business leader can become part of a much greater, worldwide effort, where how the business operates can collectively have a positive impact. In assessing "your World" look at the SDGs and see where your relevance is.

As our book illustrates, we and the leaders interviewed know that long-term sustainable success in business is best achieved where a commitment to ethical, sustainable and responsible practices represent comment aspects of the business operation. Business playing a positive role in wider society is not just the way in which a business might spend money it has made (by way of philanthropic spending), but rather it sits at the heart of how it makes its money in the first place.

> *"Business is a vital partner of most urgent societal challenges in achieving the Sustainable Development Goals. Companies can contribute through their core activities, and we ask companies everywhere to assess their impact, set ambitious goals and communicate transparently about the results."*

Ban Ki-moon, United Nations Secretary-General

More information and advice for business can be found at: http://sdgcompass.org/

The next chapter will help you decide how to start purposefully as you endeavour to build your own successful legacies.

Ask yourself the questions below. Through these and such reflections you should be able to clarify exactly how your business and you yourself are both influenced by and can in turn influence the world you occupy.

1. **What are the minimum expectations and what will your clarity of purpose allow you to exceed them on?** Appreciating the market is critical in terms of defining a distinct market offering. However the component parts of your offer manifest themselves, a clear sense of purpose should drive the brand or business offer.

2. **What will your customers pay?** You need to assess not just what people will pay for now but what else they will accommodate based upon your purpose being clearly defined and relevant to them. Will they pay a premium because of how you do business and, if so, how do you inform them?

3. **What will your competitors, partners, employees and suppliers think?** Your business depends on a supply chain and others that form part of the marketplace and therefore you need to understand their positions, manage concerns and communicate why your way of doing business will be better for all.

Next, ask yourself these questions to assess the societal expectations you will face:

1. **What are the minimum expectations within your society?** Appreciating what society expects from businesses in your sector is key. Is it particular standards of environmental management, workplace policies, access to information or something else? You must consider what these are and how to build business by going beyond them.

2. **What will your reputation aspiration be?** You must consider what you want your business to stand for, how its reputation will be built, even with those who never purchase your products.

3. **What other influencers in society are key to your wider reputation?** Your business depends on a licence to operate. You may find that there are expectations in other areas such as the public sector, links with government agendas, local public service providers that you should consider as key to building wider societal acceptance and support.

Finally, you need to be clear in understanding what you see your commitment as a purposeful leader and your business achieving in the world.

1. **What do you expect people to think?** You need to consider how you will be seen, as an innovator (or a crackpot) and feel comfortable in how you think the world will view you and react to your way of doing things.

2. **What comfort factors do you need?** You must consider what you want your business to provide you with, both materially and in terms of satisfaction, pride, status, etc. These things matter because they mark the way in which you expect society to reward you for the path you are taking.

3. **What other change will you expect in the world?** Your business will be aiming to put something of value in the world. The implications of that are that the world will change for the better, be it for the people you employ, the customers you serve or your own loved ones. Be clear in your reflection here of how you hope the world will change in this regard as a result of your business success. It is, in effect, your vision of the world you want to occupy.

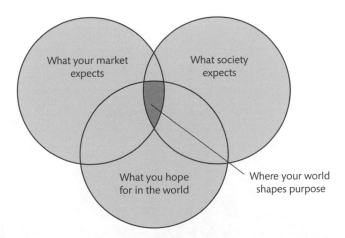

 All these points will then give you a clearer understanding of what makes up your particular world, what influences exist there and how you hope to influence it in return.

And remember, as Lord Browne said, never stop asking "What's happening on the Rialto?"

Chapter 4

Make it real

Introduction

We have seen that the purpose of a great company is its reason for being. It ensures a clear definition of the reason for its existence and how it contributes positively to the world. Purpose determines what goals a company will set and its approach and strategy for achieving them. It will determine its leadership approach and the values and beliefs that are its foundation. Such purpose is as fundamental to the success of a company as our values and beliefs are to us as individuals.

Regardless of an acceptance of this awareness, we find many people experience great difficulty in finding the means through which to progress confidently. Meeting this need is what this book is about: supporting clients and applying collective thinking and enhancement to create a simple process.

What we aim is for the resulting purpose to be enlightening, compelling and capable of inspiring and engaging all company stakeholders. This requires bonds of trust, shared values and a clear sense of direction that is achieved by a strong sense of purposefulness.

A strong corporate culture

You already understand that a company's purpose reflects its experiences and track record, including market volatilities, the character of customers and promises of quality and competence delivered as part of a covenant with stakeholders. This all forms part of a reciprocal arrangement between the company and society to contribute to human betterment.

Much of this is achieved through a strong corporate culture that encourages internal and external stakeholders to create and sustain a collective culture. Purpose is shown to be highly capable of creating such a corporate culture and long-term business success.

While leadership expert Peter Drucker is attributed with the phrase "culture eats strategy for breakfast", we like to say that "culture gets its appetite from purpose".

The practical steps

By progressing through this book, you have made the decision to apply your own purpose and shape your business as a purpose-powered one. This next critical step is how to activate it.

Purpose has become a movement and many people and institutions are articulating why all businesses should have one and what it should be about. However, far fewer are illustrating or creating realistic and practical routes to achieving that. This is partially because it appears as a relatively new phenomenon (which it isn't of course) and, secondly, because those who are propounding the gospel of purpose often can lack the practical know-how and case experience to formulate the means of change.

This is not meant as a criticism but simply an observation. The more advocates who can promote the general significance and importance the better, but it is the practical experience and support to those who wish to embrace purpose that only now is being developed by many new entries to the agenda.

 At One Hundred, our practical delivery and support of the purpose agenda over many years and across a wealth of projects for all sizes of business, as well as not-for-profits and individuals, has allowed us to capture and refine an activation process.

Although many organisations promote various rationales of what a purpose-led business should look like and how it should behave, we concentrate on allowing people to work through what their own purpose should be and how it manifests itself. That is what these next stages will allow you to do.

Let us, therefore, put aside the past's obsession with maximising shareholder value as a failed purpose and all agree with Charles Handy's suggestion that the true position is less definitive and clear-cut. It should depend on the individual company and what it is aspiring to achieve.

He concluded: "Business purpose is something that each company must define for itself because it is, at its heart, a community (versus a property)

. . . whose principal purpose is to fulfil itself, to grow and to develop to the best that it can be, given always that every other corporation is free to do the same."

At Countrywide, Alison Platt says:

> *"I see the outputs of a purpose-powered business as totally aligned to the outcomes that shareholders look for in terms of returns.*
>
> *"It's about value creation over time through building a better company more aligned to the needs of its customers and its employees. This creates organic growth and increases returns through continually improved process, removal of error and waste and innovation focused on customers' desires."*

Four simple elements

The following is a simple structure that you can look towards developing for yourself. It looks for four simple self-assessments:

- **Purpose:** why you are in business – your rationale to help people and the world.

- **Ambition:** what you wish to be, in order to and as a result of achieving your purpose.

- **Commitment:** how your business will operate while achieving your purpose.

- **Strategic aims:** what you need hope to achieve in your powered business.

Simple as these four key elements might seem, companies and leaders sometimes find it difficult to create the clarity of thinking to achieve such definition. We advise them to see it as a combined eco-structure as illustrated within the following figure and with illustrative strategic objectives. In getting business to aim towards what we call the "on target" purpose diagram it requires them to undertake our activation methodology – to make it real.

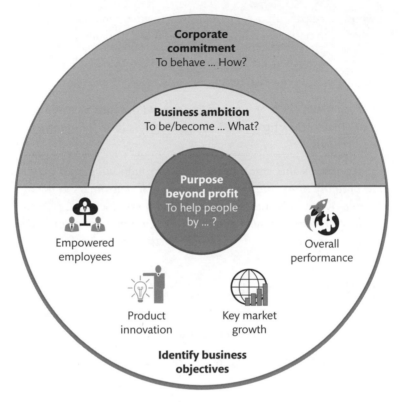

"On target" purpose diagram

To make purpose real within your business, you will need to undertake self-assessment to populate a diagram such as the one above. It will then reflect your purpose in its entirety on one page. You will be able to create your own "on target" purpose diagram.

The key to populating this is developing the appropriate thought process leading to it. The course of thinking and the clarity of why you behave in certain ways, and why a team feels the way it does, are open to straightforward analysis.

The purpose that emerges is part of our natural and continual quest for furthering existence. The purpose of doing something is what the world is built upon. We need to embrace our purpose and then manage it to create the value in it as the key component upon which our world relies.

How it happens in practice

At Boots Opticians, Ben Fletcher says the company had a major advantage and head start, being able to use the purpose with which the larger Boots Group was, essentially, developed in the mid to late nineteenth century by Jesse Boot, building on the roots of his family's herbal medicine shop in Nottingham.

> *"We've been really explicit, internally and externally, about our purpose in a different way over the last three years, and we do so as British opticians in the context of a bigger business. Boots was founded with a fantastic purpose and was an incredible innovation-driven business. The very simple idea of Jesse Boot was that healthcare should be accessible to everyone regardless of their means, essentially."*

Boots Opticians added to this inherited purpose by crafting individualised purpose statements, such as "We commit to enrich the life of every person," and "We are a health-led optician and care about a whole lot more."

> *"The words especially don't have to mean anything to anyone else outside of the business, but what it did was provide the start point for everything that followed. What we didn't do was start off, for example, on a strategy-setting exercise.*
>
> *"We started off on a purpose exercise and got really clear on that purpose statement and what it meant to us and then said: 'If that is what we are going to be, what are the where-to-play and how-to-win choices that flow from that? What would the business look like if we lived this in every way?'"*

At Lego, Judith Houston, the company's former business conduct and ethics manager, had a similar experience.

> *"You are indoctrinated, for lack of a better word, with the history of Lego and not just the history but the values of Lego. Most of its values are about creativity, quality and not necessarily what I would call ethical values, but I think the ethical side of things is just implicit in all of those. It's about making the best thing you can for the children. When they*

talk about money and targets, sales targets, they don't actually talk about money, they talk about the number of children we want to reach "

Sir Mike Rake at BT Group argues that a good illustration of the factors behind the ability to frame purpose is that which is being advocated by "Blueprint for Better Business".

"You have to treat your employees, customers, suppliers, community and environment fairly. If you do those things consciously, not as part of a CSR sub-committee but as part of the DNA of a company so that is your approach to life, you will have a successful business.

"There will be things that will happen in a fast-moving world but, if you bear these principles in mind, all the academic research shows that, other things being equal, people will be attracted to the brands with the better reputations."

Varied approaches

Other organisations are also championing slightly varied approaches with different yet similarly aligned objectives.

In the UK, in 2016, Business in the Community, the traditional champion of CSR, issued its first working party report on purpose, while the B Corporation movement is spreading around the globe. 2016 also saw the British Government consult One Hundred Partners and others on the mission-based business agenda.

This is all very encouraging, but to activate and to achieve this remarkable shift requires a combination of critical thinking alongside a confident set of steps leading to successful purpose identification. The natural course of taking such steps lends itself nicely to the analogy of stepping stones in a river: slightly uneasy, the surrounding influences, like water swirling around, potentially distracting.

Other steps might appear possible as short cuts or more easily achieved, but the reality is that, unless you keep to the path, such distractions can kill your quest for purpose stone dead. Just think of all the times you have started to consider your personal or business strategy, only to have distractions get in the way.

Just about everyone will have started such analysis at one point or another, but rarely managed to give themselves the chance to succeed. Why? Because there is a constant struggle from the moment you start to extract yourself from day-to-day distractions, to be pulled back by the very things you need to distance your thinking from.

The vested interests of third parties, cultural norms or societal expectations, alongside competitors, financial concerns, staffing morale and all sorts of other influences, are stacked to maintain the status quo and block new thinking.

Framing an agreed purpose helps line up leaders and staff behind common objectives, resulting in quicker decisions and better unity.

Alison Platt continues:

"Clarity of purpose enables speedier and more aligned decision making. One example at Countrywide would be our review of a large takeover target whose values are very different from ours.

"Despite attractive short-term financials, we knew we would ultimately destroy value as there was no alignment of purpose of values. We didn't do the deal and that proved to be a very good decision.

"The key challenge for leaders is that timescales and the demands for short-term profit can get in the way. Leaders need patience and nerve and they need to invest time in taking shareholders with them."

Having provided you with a few indications of what people consider, we will now lay out the process.

If you are an individual entrepreneur, perhaps thinking of creating a business for the first time, or even self-employed or a micro-business, the temptation may be to undertake this yourself and on your own. Although we would agree the need for you to enter such a process with some pre-thinking and clarity in your own mind, we would recommend strongly that others are involved in your process, be they friends and associates, even if you don't have employees as such.

For conventional businesses, leadership teams, boards and groups you rely upon should be selected to undertake this with you. There are practical limitations on how many you should involve and how such sessions are run.

 This we will detail further in this chapter as a checklist and aide memoire to making the process work.

The purpose definition

First, let us clarify our start point. We take the "on target" purpose diagram on page 86 and deconstruct it. We create what we call a canvas, made up of four large pieces of paper set next to each other on the wall, with the following headings:

- Our purpose.

- Our ambition.

- Our commitment.

- Our objectives.

True to our direction about focus, the notes that are added to each sheet should be measured, agreed, clear and carefully crafted. These charts should not have hundreds of notes stuck all over them with wacky ideas and single words like "innovation". Such stuff is for different priorities.

So, in managing the sessions, give one person the task of creating smart Post-it notes that reflect a key point you have created collectively.

This means that at the end of the day, you will not be confronted simply with a mass of messy Post-it notes with no logical thought to them. Rather, you will have captured a succinct group of key statements from which you can craft your purpose statement (more about that later) and your strategic objectives.

As pointers for your discussions, you should be considering these four master questions:

1. Your purpose: why you are in business.

This is your appreciation of why you exist. You know from reading previous chapters that you will enter this process knowing your sense of personal purpose, understanding the world around you and having a sense of the opportunity ahead of you. Knowing where you are to start with is, therefore, a critical piece of understanding, allowing you to enter the process confidently.

You already have acknowledged already that your prime purpose is not to make money or become a millionaire. These things could, should, may, happen if you prove successful but the purpose needs a nobler rationale.

If you are in healthy catering you may wish to see your purpose as "provide people with nutritious, healthy food to help them live long, happy lives". If you are at an airline, it might be you wish to "bring people, cultures and the world together in comfort and safety".

They are just ideas but they are human-oriented and confer a sense of nobility on your business beyond simply seeing people as a revenue stream.

2. Your ambition: what you wish to become.

This second question is to be clear about what type of business you are aiming to become. This switches your thinking to asking what your over-arching vision is. What performance do you see being illustrative of succeeding against your purpose? What scale will you have to become, where will you need to be based, how many people do you consider you will need?

When you enter the analysis, and via the tools we share below, you will need to consider what the current situation is and how it shapes your views of the future.

In some instances, for example, you may consider you do not wish to be the largest, or have more branches, in order to best achieve your purpose. All this needs to be considered. It will allow you to move on to define the key strategic objectives that which will be necessary to move you from where you are to where you wish to be. Having done so, you will be able to move on to a clear purposeful path.

3. The commitment: how you define the character of your business.

Determine the promise you are making to anyone who is involved in the business in respect of what your purpose stands for. You need to determine the values set and what you believe in, create an understanding of the benefits that will accrue from being a part of the business and, finally, consider the personality you wish your business to express. This latter may vary from contemporary, relaxed, flexible through to traditional, formal and structured. No personality is better than the other; it is simply what is right to achieve your purpose.

This is obviously part of the web and weave of the culture you wish to engender in your business. It is also in this area of self-assessment where you consider competitors, collaborators and customer perspectives of you and what you are trying to achieve.

By putting yourself in their mind's eye, you can determine the way in which your commitment around purpose manifests itself in the way you engage with them. How you will commit to deal with them in a way that illustrates your vision of the business as it will manifest itself with third parties.

4. Your objectives: what you need to work towards initially.

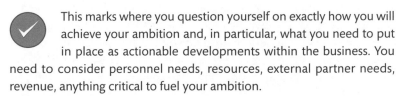 This marks where you question yourself on exactly how you will achieve your ambition and, in particular, what you need to put in place as actionable developments within the business. You need to consider personnel needs, resources, external partner needs, revenue, anything critical to fuel your ambition.

Although they become the management mechanisms to monitor your progress, they also become important practical aspects of how you are choosing to progress as a purposeful business to your team who will inevitably will be working towards them as specific, well-understood objectives.

Once completed, you will have the answers to the complete picture and can put the pieces of the jigsaw in place, creating your own "on target" purpose diagram, a simple reflection of what your business is now about.

These four groups of questions are designed to allow you to think about your current position as a purpose-led business. The answers can, possibly, appear too succinct to have great meaning, but the opposite is actually the case. The clearer and more focused these can be, the better they are at defining the purpose-driven ambition to be understood and embraced by colleagues and other stakeholders.

This process will allow everyone involved to appreciate your position and create greater understanding of the ultimate purpose of the time and energy you spend doing what you do.

Running a successful purpose definition workshop

Many people come to One Hundred having had lots of workshop experiences over many years, covering a multitude of topics and facilitated in different styles. Some people like them, some loathe them; whatever the position, we all will have experienced the good, the bad and the ugly.

We pride ourselves on creating an alternative that makes significant progress in a day and has been appreciated universally by our clients as different, meaningful and capable of fast forwarding their development. Our house style is based on our team: our character, humour and ability to probe and ask respectful, but difficult, questions.

We cannot be in every workshop you run, but we can share how we do it, the tools we use and the pitfalls to avoid. This section on running a workshop culminates in details of how you can define your own purpose statement with good examples from others.

With the right people in the room and the right motivation, by undertaking the following you can move yourself to the aim of completing your own "on target" purpose diagram by the end of the day.

Bear in mind the following:

- Understand what you are attempting to achieve.

- Use a "canvas" model you can create easily.

- Think who will join you in exploring and defining this.

- Consider the practical things that will make it run smoothly.

Introduction to doing a workshop

Lots of people do lots of brainstorming. Such sessions can become really dynamic and the various methodologies are as numerous as the number of ideas that can be generated. However, our experience tells us more structure is required.

We are not going to advocate that walls are plastered with hundreds of Post-it notes, or that there are no such things as bad ideas, or that the workshop is a safe place, etc, etc. These things work elsewhere but here we want focus. We have big questions that need sensible ideas, critical thinking, challenge and a clarity of thinking which many of the often-quoted workshop doctrines work against.

Last year we supported a client who, over the course of a year, had run various workshops with third-party facilitators to derive a solution to an issue. They came to us at the 12-month point with 160 different ideas. They had lost the ability to see the wood for the trees. We analysed what they had done and within a month we created eight new alternatives as a "long shortlist", all strategically vision-enhancing and purpose-orientated. Within a further week they had selected three for further development and within three weeks of that they selected "the one".

Unfortunately, we hear a lot from clients about weak facilitation they have witnessed before, silly warm-ups, games and processes where time is lost, ideas aren't scrutinised and no progress is made. You don't have that time to waste and, although we are not against people enjoying the process – we inject humour and fun as we go through a day – this is serious business requiring absolute clarity of thought and progress towards the results you want from the day. This is what you need to do to get that clarity of purpose.

Here are some tips on preparing for a workshop:

- **When and where?** We recommend identifying a full free day. It needs to be when your key contributors, management team, stakeholders and whoever you wish to participate can confirm they can clear that time and commit fully to the process. This needs you to emphasise the significance of this workshop. It will be the day you transform the future of the business.

- **Schedule it properly.** Make arrangements for lunch and other refreshments. Ideally, we recommend you host business workshops off-site. A fresh environment from alternative location business meeting facilities through to a hotel or even private home helps separate the current business distractions from the process.

- **Which participants?** You yourself need to determine who you want there. If you have a senior management team, then they need to be top of the list. Ideally, you shouldn't try and exceed half a dozen or so participants. That can be a challenge and may lead to multiple, concurrent workshops if you simply must have more than that, but our advice is keep it to a core nucleus capable of supporting your thinking.

- **Participant preparation.** Set their expectations by telling them they don't have to do anything in advance, except to come prepared to consider what sort of business they want to work in, which companies they admire (regardless of sector) and why. If you know you have individuals who may be challenged by the concept of purpose, then spend time before trying to make sure they appreciate its significance. You cannot afford time on the day with people who fundamentally disagree with the concept. That is not what this workshop sets out to address. You need your participants to be willing, enthusiastic and eager to follow your lead.

- **Visual aids.** Below we provide a form template to copy. You will also require pens, Post-it notes, spare paper for ad hoc notes and, if available, flip charts.

- **Record keeper.** You require someone who can participate in the discussion if you wish but whose responsibility on the day is to complete a set of notes. We are not suggesting minutes, but you need a record and the notes will support the visual record – we recommend you use a phone camera to capture your Post-it note outputs for future reference.

- **Pre-reading.** If you have the ability and lead-in time, ask them to read this book or at least mark key sections you wish them to understand.

- **The room.** We all know that behaviour is shaped by the environment we are in. Avoid a formal square "boardroom" style table or room layout. If you feel it can help inspire thinking, then bring in magazines, photos, create a mood board of images that may relate to your key themes or things that illustrate the world in which you operate or your competitor's approach. Put fruit, not just chocolate, on the table and make sure the lighting, temperature and chairs are comfortable. You may bring in some of your products, or Lego bricks or moulding clay to fiddle with, but whatever your style, everything should be designed to free up and stimulate the positive in your people.

- **Set the rules.** Explain and reiterate on the day. All phones and email devices should be switched off and used only during refreshment breaks and, if possible, sparingly (you want people in the purpose "zone" away from distractions). Let people know any other aspects you feel important to set the tone you want, such as dress, when phones can be looked at, courtesy during debates, etc.

Making it work

The best way we know to encourage analysis that makes sense and fosters confidence is to approach each key question as a three-stage conversation:

- **Explain:** start by explaining clearly the major question, what it means to you, the level of thought you are expecting. If possible, give examples from purpose businesses you admire to bring the theme of that question to life. Make sure you are happy that your team are happy and understand what you are hoping to get out of this session.

- **Engage:** have everyone have their say. Get them to start naturally or, if they don't, nominate and ask around the room, but don't let one person (including yourself) dominate the conversation. Try to encourage a natural flow of ideas as if you were doing so in a relaxed environment.

- **Reflect:** when you are within 15 minutes of the end of the session, lead a discussion of where you think you are at. Reflect what has been said, the conclusions made and the main Post-it notes you have up on the board. Understand if people are stuck, consider what parts were challenging. Ask people if they have learned anything new or realised something they have forgotten to contribute. Illustrate your own conclusions by explaining your insights and observations on their comments, thereby demonstrating that these answers are shared.

In this way, you will initiate, collectively create and then evaluate together before moving on to the next session.

More things to consider before you start:

- **Be the leader:** you are leading both the business and the workshop. Do not shy away from ensuring that the workshop runs in the direction you want it to. You need to accept the ability to be challenged but, if you have a purpose vision for the business, your job as leader is to lead the others on to that path. However that clarity of purpose may be shaped, whatever language may evolve from the process, you still set the course for the day. It is pointless if you spend the day debating with someone that the purpose of the business is to make money.

- **Consider external facilitation:** although it is perfectly possible and appropriate to have a well-run workshop and facilitate it yourself, if resources and contacts allow, you may choose to bring in either an external facilitator or find a trusted individual with the right skill-set internally to undertake the role. The role of facilitator on the day is to be responsible for leading the progress of the workshop, being concerned about timings, being a fair voice for all present and other aspects of making things run smoothly. Ultimately, the role is to make sure that participants are focused and productive. You may find it hard to do that role, as well as participate fully or be not simply "the boss".

- **Be prepared to fail:** there may be an occasion within the day where your train of thinking might lead to a dead end or your team fails to follow your own lead. We have yet to find a situation that actually could be described as failure but there may be that point where you stall. Be prepared and ready to stop, get everyone to take an unscheduled break, fresh air or whatever. During that five or ten minutes, reflect yourself on how to circumvent the blockage. By being prepared to accept the need to stop, consider and appreciate the situation fully, you will come up with a new way forward.

- **Finish on a high:** at the end of the day you will want to finish with a strong closing message that emphasises the main achievements of the day. Therefore, you need to summarise strongly, thanking people for their efforts but also offering the opportunity for final questions at the end.

Think before you start how you will summarise, stressing the importance of what you have jointly contributed to. Explain that you will now take the notes and pictures of the canvas to digest into language capable of populating the "on target" purpose diagram. Hopefully, if it has gone well, much of the finished language will be there already and simply will require some slight refinement and the collation into the diagram.

Management on the day

If the above is applied, you should start the day free from distractions by stating the purpose of the workshop. Show the "on target" purpose diagram and explain that you are aiming to get consensus to create a draft of it by the end of the day. Also, explain the canvas areas of questioning. Detail when breaks will occur and how you will manage and facilitate the questioning which is appropriate to your corporate culture. The following is a typical agenda for such a workshop.

09.00 – 09.15 **Refreshments on arrival**

09.15 – 09.45 **Introductions and objectives.** Explain the sections of the "canvas" on the wall and the crib sheets (see below). Allow time for questions and queries. Iron out any concerns over process at this point.

09.45 – 11.00 **Session 1: The purpose vision.** Describe what you think purpose means to you, the business and the world in which you operate. Run a first set of questioning around this to fill in the "Your purpose" section of the canvas. What does the business do? What is the business aiming to achieve for people generally?

11.00 – 11.15 **Refreshments and coffee break**

11.15 – 12.45 **Session 2: Business ambition.** From the finish point of clarity at the end of the first session ask what the business needs to look like to achieve its aims. This is setting out the type of organisation best placed to achieve its purpose. Consider all questions, as suggested above, covering such matters as size, profile, brand recognition, locations, etc.

Before you break for lunch, recap on both sessions. Be upbeat and highlight and celebrate any thinking breakthroughs that may have occurred.

12.45 – 13.30 **Lunch.** Phone calls and emails may be checked, if they must!

13.30 – 15.00 **Session 3: Commitment.** Your particular unique proposition. Ask how you will operate, what your values are and what you will do differently. What will be your way of behaving that will reflect to all stakeholders your purpose? What will be your corporate

---

personality? How does the brand express itself? Who is the business particularly relevant to or focused on and what will be their experience from you?

15.00 – 15.15 **Break**

15.15 – 16.45 **Session 4: Strategic objectives** ● Refocus people after the break by reminding them of the distance travelled and the key observations you have made previously. Now set out clear specific objectives that you feel will be required to make the business fit for purpose. These should be manageable and make sense in a timely fashion. They could include anything from a new IT system to staff working practices. This section can be a very broad brainstorm requiring some ruthless prioritisation afterwards.

16.45 – 17.00 **Summary and conclusions** ● End on a high. Make sure people feel happy and excited about the purpose and their contribution in shaping it. Explain when the summary action notes based on the canvas will be shared. Explain any process matters, such as whether people think of something they wish to share after the event.

17.00 **End**

The follow-up

Once you have finished the workshop, you will need to review the results, considering the wider aspects of the thinking you conducted before. This will include your own perspective on purpose, the defined operating world, your competitive landscape and anything that emerged from your workshop that you feel requires further consideration or research.

Take care to ensure that, as you begin to craft the key statements and draw up the "on target" purpose diagram, you don't inadvertently discard components or matters that you wish to discard but others may wish to be included (and therefore may not understand why you have discarded them). The content needs to be shared back with the participants either individually (via email) or collectively for comments, reactions and agreement.

Once you have your defined statements, draw them up and present them to your audience. Be clear on why you have used language or emphasis. To convey the full meaning of the words you have chosen, augment them in your feedback as you see fit, with definitions, images and similar words.

Compare these attributes to those of the competition to show how customers should understand the differentiation of your purpose over others.

In doing this, the most pressing and singularly important question will be defined; namely, your purpose statement. This most important start point, the work you did right at the start of the canvas is your public evocation of the difference you are trying to make in the world.

It is so important it is worthy of separate consideration. This advice ideally should be applied in addressing the "Our purpose" question but, more than likely, you will wish to do this yourself beforehand to help lead your thinking in the direction you feel is right for your organisation.

Getting to the purpose statement

Judith Houston at Lego says:

 "The first thing about your statement is obviously that you have to identify a very specific purpose. It sounds silly, but identify and be very clear about it and articulate it clearly, and make it simple.

"The second thing you must have is something people can buy into. If you have a purpose, and it's your purpose and no one else buys into it, then it may not have the effect or the impact that it would if someone, or everyone, can buy into it."

When planning the Eden Project, Sir Tim Smit says he had one simple idea.

"I simply wanted to create a place that is incredibly theatrical. A place that emphasised human dependence on the natural world and, to a degree, would encapsulate 'awe', a word that is horribly abused, but which it is essential for us to rediscover the true meaning of."

For your business purpose statement, it is also your current brand position, how it is viewed, its reputation, recognition, strengths and weaknesses that will inform the process. It is your sense of purpose objectives, what you wish to see changed in the world and what you can improve.

Robin Wight, president of advertising combine The Engine Group, recalls helping to launch mobile phone network Orange in 1994 with the slogan "The future's bright, the future's Orange". They had clarity of purpose, understood where they were and where their brand was.

> *"That wasn't particularly about ethics. It wasn't particularly about sustainability, but what it was about when we looked at the things that it offered was a conviction about serving customers better. A conviction brand is a brand with an inner belief about the way things are.*

> *"What I call a 'confection brand' is a brand that goes and asks consumers questions in the normal way. It does the normal research, and ends up producing the same product as everybody else, because they've all asked the same questions to the same people.*

> *"The most successful brands don't work like that. They leap ahead of consumers, they have a viewpoint about the way the world should be and they make their world that way. If they've got their hunch right, they're much more successful."*

Taking One Hundred Partners as an example, we say:

"We help activate purpose in others, supporting clients to maximise performance and their positive impact on the world." Our shorthand tag line is:

> *"Activating purpose for good."*

 So how do you go about determining a purpose and its purpose statement?

Crafting the purpose statement

A purpose statement alone doesn't make a purpose-driven company. The company's purpose statement tells people why it exists, but the effectiveness of a purpose-driven business is illustrated not by the words, but by the behaviours as they exemplify the purpose. These values and practices are defined in the following sections but, as important as the statement is, it cannot be everything.

Relevant and authentic

A good purpose must be directly relevant and appropriate to how you earn your income if it is to be authentic and reflective of your core competencies and what you are saying to the world.

Products and services can and will change over time, particularly as technology and customer expectations develop. If your stated purpose was to provide mass mobility to working people, you may have started by making bicycles in the early twentieth century, but adopted the petrol engine by the mid-century and may now have turned electric and be shifting to driverless.

Your purpose will have remained relevant – no doubt with the same core engineering and business skills, but the product has changed. The "why" is the same and the "what" is different.

Acknowledging the world

Thinking back to Chapter 3 on understanding the world, your purpose must also be part of the bigger picture and the factors affecting your sector.

Take an ethical coffee business. The minimum expectation now is to have a Fairtrade coffee alternative for purchase. Leading companies such as Pret a Manger and Starbucks go further with specifically identified growers, cooperative support programmes, carbon offsetting, employee volunteering and a raft of other responsible practices that have set a norm within the sector far beyond the minimum.

If you are striving to be at the leading edge, you must be alert not only to the normal and minimal market influences but also to where the expectation is heading. If you are pioneering, you will be setting the precedent and leading those expectations.

Undertake a reality check

You may be leading a company with a purpose statement in place, in which case it will either be working for you or not. You may be leading a new initiative where you want to craft an all-encompassing and motivating purpose statement and this will help you.

You may also be in a really strong purpose-driven business that has never needed a statement. We have come across a minority of these. But, even if this is the case, when asked, such leaders will always have a set of words they use to describe what they do. So they effectively do have a purpose statement, even if they don't acknowledge it or hang it over the door.

Says Robin Wight of The Engine Group:

"We adopt status behaviour because that's the way we're wired up biologically. We may find different ways of expressing it. Our wiring requires us to find a way to signal our genetic fitness. That is what status at the biological level is. It might be shoes or sneakers. It may be we can make them more sustainable rainforest shoes. The ways which status expresses itself will change, but it may not always be conspicuous consumption. It could be conspicuous non-consumption."

Put passion into it

To progress, you need to define the purpose of your business in a succinct, hopefully uniquely engaging, fashion. So how do you do this? As we have shown, passion in purpose in business is led by people of passion around their own purpose. So, the number one issue is to find your "purpose passion". What do you care most about and what do you want your company to care most for?

Second, but most important, we have seen time and time again that the success of purpose-driven businesses is defined by the overlap between three things: what you are passionate about, what you are good at and what the world needs.

So, what does the world need? And what are you good at? Once you have these in mind, purpose definition needs to be bold and ambitious. What exactly will all your efforts do to create a better world?

Use simple language

The most ambitious of dreams can be summed up in simple language and this is what good purpose statements are. Many of the examples that you will read below illustrate how good purpose statements combine brevity with ambition.

Making it stick

This process, if it doesn't come naturally, needs some proper time with some hard thinking and possibly trawling through others to get inspiration. The language and words you use are important and it could take days to be sure it works across various groups and stakeholders. It will challenge you but it will be business-defining.

Once you have your purpose refined, you will have laid the first foundation stone of a better and more successful brand. Stick it on the wall, use it to build a vision, live it and breathe it.

A warning

Words of caution: a business purpose isn't just a tagline. One of the risks we see is that some public relations and marketing agencies have started to champion purpose and however genuinely interested they are in the subject, their perspective inevitably is shaped by it becoming simply a communications device.

Although that is important, true purpose requires a commitment from across an organisation, to embed purpose into practices and behaviours as well as the decision making process.

Some effective purpose statements

Nourishing families so they can flourish and thrive – **Kellogg's**

To help people manage risk and recover from the hardship of unexpected loss – **International Airlines Group**

To put smiles on the faces of everyone we touch – **Nintendo**

To create a better everyday life for the many people – **IKEA**

To bring inspiration and innovation to every athlete in the world – **Nike**

To inspire and nurture the human spirit – one person, one cup and one neighborhood at a time – **Starbucks**

To refresh the world in mind, body and spirit. To inspire moments of optimism and happiness through our brands and actions. To create value and make a difference – **Coca-Cola**

To embrace the human spirit and let it fly – **Virgin Atlantic**

To help people all over the world make progress in their lives through learning – **Pearson**

To promote global wellness and nutrition while building a sustainable environment and honouring our role in society from farm to the family – **Campbell's Soup**

Bringing health through food to as many people as possible – **Danone**

To inspire and develop children to think creatively, reason systematically and release their potential to shape their own future, experiencing the endless human possibility – **Lego**

To achieve the best outcome for the pensioners on whose behalf we invest – **Hermes Investment Management**

To improve the quality of human life by enabling people to do more, feel better and live longer – **GlaxoSmithKline**

> Improving people's lives through meaningful innovation
> – **Philips**
>
> Together we will make beauty sustainable. Together we will
> make sustainability beautiful – **L'Oréal**
>
> Making sustainable living commonplace – **Unilever**
>
> Delivering experiences that our customers love, for life
> – **Jaguar Land Rover**

You are now going to write your own purpose statement. Here is our suggested process:

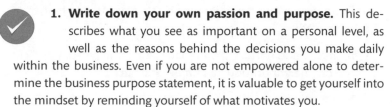

1. **Write down your own passion and purpose.** This describes what you see as important on a personal level, as well as the reasons behind the decisions you make daily within the business. Even if you are not empowered alone to determine the business purpose statement, it is valuable to get yourself into the mindset by reminding yourself of what motivates you.

   What inspires you to do the work you do? What changes do you want to create in the world? What gets you out of bed each morning? Evaluating what you see as your purpose in life allows you to recognise what you hope to achieve through your business and the work you do every day.

2. **Create your world reference point.** This is the point that talks to both you and your customers. It will help you position exactly what you are trying to do in the world and help shape the language required to do so effectively. Do these words reflect something people can feel about your business?

3. **Define the values of the business.** These will be behind the scenes but could well be reflective in your purpose statement, if appropriate. Whatever values are within the business will need to be in the DNA of the statement. Many businesses do not put enough consideration into the value questions, which creates difficulties in engaging with their audiences.

If we take One Hundred Partners as an example, we are unusual because we are one of a few established agencies created specifically to promote purpose, rather than emerging from a PR, marketing or auditing background.

In creating our purpose statement, we fused the learning of both our founder with his not for profit experience and his cofounders from commercial backgrounds in a way that embraced the character of how we operate and why, the values behind the business and the clarity of what we do.

We came to the following conclusions:

1. We are all about helping people on purpose to do good.

2. We base our work on ethical and sustainable thinking.

3. We don't just talk about it, we are renowned for delivering it.

4. We are committed to doing the best we can for all.

5. We care about people.

6. We care about the planet's sustainability.

7. We believe in the ability to build responsible, prosperous businesses.

This meant that the following words were identified as key: purpose, activation, good, people, planet and prosperity.

This led directly to our purpose:

> **"We help activate purpose in others, supporting clients to maximise performance and their positive impact on the world."**

Our shorthand tag line is:

> **"Activating purpose for good."**

 It works. If you ask our clients they will tell you this is exactly what we do, is what we are valued for and what we are passionate about.

Once the statement exists, it needs to be reflective of the culture and practices of the business.

As Judith Houston says:

> **"I've never told someone that I work for Lego and had a negative reaction. It's been a positive reaction – a happy, enthusiastic one and a smile. It evokes memories and then people say: 'I used to do this with my father or grandfather' and that they still get a box of Lego every year.**

"There are a lot of feelings associated with Lego and it's one of the reasons why it is successful. A lot of us were brought up with Lego and when we have children, we want them to have the same experience."

Lego has been building on its purpose for 85 years and it can take time for purpose to become as embedded in culture as it is at the Danish company. But now is the day to start.

Chapter summary

You have now progressed through the self-assessment. You are prepared to define your purpose, your commitment, your ambition and the strategic objectives. You can start to populate your "on target" purpose diagram as the go-to summary of what you are about.

 The next chapter is about creating a purposeful culture and the practices on which it is built. It takes the strategy and makes it real. It evokes how you and your colleagues will live and lead the business and is where purpose will jump off the page into day-to-day operations.

Chapter 5

Create your culture

Introduction

Although policies can be important in creating purposeful businesses, practices are much more influential in shaping that culture.

The culture of your organisation, how you invest in creating it and how others embrace it will, fundamentally, be the single biggest factor in determining your success. Businesses can have the best strategies in the world but if their people don't agree with them, they will fail.

In this chapter we will consider how such a culture is created through practices rather than specifically listing the type of policies one might establish.

The meaning of culture

Let's be clear what we are talking about. The word "culture" has three meanings:

- Literally, it refers to tilling the soil, growing, meaning cultivation.

- As a metaphor, culture is used in respect of training or refining the mind, meaning civilisation.

- Over the past few decades, a broader metaphor has become ubiquitous: derived from anthropology and denoting our collective behaviours, thinking and feelings. Culture in this sense is defined as "the collective programming of the mind that distinguishes the members of one group or category of people from others" (Hofstede et al).

So what we are trying to create in a purposeful business is a universally appreciated culture, where people have a collective state of mind, knowing why the business exists, what it does, where within it they understand their role to be and why they are proud of being a part.

It is where, through a combined emotional bond, the group, your team, your business, has a tangible sense of unity and positive interaction between themselves and with customers, suppliers and others. It is that sense of the positive that amplifies purpose in your business to the world.

This "culture" has to be recognised as a construct, a product of our individual creativity and imagination. The issue is that it will emerge either by default or design and, whether positive or negative, it will be directly present from verbal statements and other measurable behaviours through to hidden and less obvious actions.

Creating a strong purposeful culture

To ensure success, it is vital to give thought to helping design what is in your mind as the ideal purposeful culture for your business. That is the golden thread that will permeate every aspect of your operation and shape the business you want.

How you create this culture will be based on your own clarity of purpose and your ability to voice it and then walk the talk, with your personal practices setting the tone and the expectations and standards of others.

In managing this, it is best to keep in mind that people are most interested in why you are doing this – your own motivation. You will then need to explain how you will do it and then what you will do. It is important to have these clear and distinct in your own mind. Then you can start building the practices and the culture.

Culture is critical, You can't have a successful purpose strategy unless your culture is hungry for it. Your culture is your recipe for success because it is what will drive recruitment of the best long-term client and customer relationships and performance.

What will make up your particular culture may well be quirky, shaped by your products or brand characteristics, but equally by your location, traditions and the good practice you have been a part of elsewhere. However particular to you, it must be fit for purpose and so how you invest in creating it and how others embrace it will be key to determining your success.

Establishing purposeful practices

The next step, therefore, is to create purposeful practices within your organisation. This is not about writing lots of policies, it's about establishing practices. To create a purposeful business, you need a purposeful culture, but to create a purposeful culture you need purposeful practices.

Timothy Melgund at Paperchase explains the difference.

> *"When we bought the business in a management buyout in 1996, one of the main drivers was that we wanted to make it a very nice place to work and we wanted to look after the team that was going to drive the business forward in a way that was better than they could get elsewhere.*

> *"We were only six people but in the head office at the time, we set ourselves up as being an employer that looked after people. But as a business gets bigger, trying to hold on to that small company ethic is one of the hardest things to do. As a business grows and you start to lose absolute involvement with every part of it, the process can start to take over from the purpose.*

> *"Part of the magic is to keep hold of the purpose and not let the process push it into a different shape. That's something we have really tried to do."*

Purpose is what shapes corporate culture and the character of the business and it is much stronger than simply a set of corporate policies. Purpose power is effectively realised not by people being attracted by what policies are in place but by how people behave, the sense of mission they are on and the collective ideals. Ask yourself: are people drawn to your organisation because of what you stand for?

Values and purpose for stakeholder relationships

How are your values and purpose applicable to how you operate with your key stakeholders? Being clear about these will attract people who share them. It creates loyalty of association and employees prepared to go that much further. Not surprisingly, this is the common cultural basis of charities and in many ways business can learn from this in shaping corporate cultures.

 Imagine what you are aspiring to create as the culture of your organisation. How will it look and feel if everyone in it has made a conscious decision to join you on your purposeful ambition? Will there be a tangible sense within the company that they knowingly committed to your purpose in order to achieve something bigger than simply the monthly pay cheque?

Of course not everyone will embrace that and you will find you then probably don't want them working for you, but building such teams can be incredibly powerful and satisfying.

Hans Laessoe, senior director of strategic risk management at Lego, says:

"We've had people who thought the culture was idiotic and that we made some silly choices and they found a company that would fit them better. We also had people that thought: 'Hey guys, you got it wrong, it's about making money'. They would be frozen out and fired, because they do not match the company.

"It may be naïve, it may be stupid, it may be whatever, but we're not in it for the money. The purpose of the company is to acquire and develop and build different models. When we're talking about success, our strategic aim for 2022 and 2032 is not about money. It's not about profits. It's not about sales. It's about reaching, in 2022, 150 million kids around the world, and 300 million kids around the world by 2032."

Establish strong values and compliance

Now think about the stakeholders that are relevant and then ask and define some principles or values about how you will behave.

It should be obvious that, regardless of which stakeholder group you are assessing, your values must be consistent. You cannot, for example, treat your staff members with great integrity if you decide you will compromise that integrity with suppliers.

You also then need to ensure that anyone representing your business appreciates that they need to adopt and adhere to these values as well. If they don't accept that, then you cannot create a consistent values-driven culture, which is what a purpose-driven business requires.

You may be starting a company from scratch or looking at shifting an existing business into a purpose-driven one. The latter doesn't allow you to select everyone afresh and it's difficult always to get new recruitment right. Therefore, the practices you either introduce or apply already are critical components of setting the parameters of behaviour within the purpose-driven agenda.

When a company moves into a new defined purpose, it needs to be appreciated by those leading the change that, if anyone doesn't accept the purpose and what it means, they may need to move on. As the purpose is non-negotiable, neither is it a matter of choice for employees to determine whether they are in or out.

By establishing the purpose and how it manifests itself in the business, people will self-determine whether they wish to be a part of it. If they don't – and simply swim against the tide – robust management must be applied.

Sometimes, it is obvious that employees should be fired as they contravene policies or even break laws. Will King, founder of shaving challenger brand King of Shaves recalls:

 "We once had a sales manager who tied us up with deals worth hundreds of thousands of pounds on the basis that they were cash deals. He was very excited about a £100,000 order from Nigeria that was to be paid in cash. We said that isn't how we do things and our bank is also going to question that transaction.

"Honesty is the best way to build a business with longevity and it expresses the values, especially when you have got your surname on the letterhead and packaging. My guiding principle is to treat others how I would like to be treated and when people behave in a way that they said they wouldn't, or you said in your values that they shouldn't, you have to take out that relationship."

It can be harder to act when dissent from a company's purpose is actually within employment contracts. But it can be just as damaging to a company's core values and mission if such staff are left in place and dissonance is allowed to spread.

At Intuit, Brad Smith says:

> *"Not complying with our core values is usually the fastest way that someone doesn't make it in this company and, very often, if there's a value when people stumble, it's winning together.*
>
> *"We believe a player that makes a team great is worth more than just a great player. We'll sometimes hire people who are incredibly smart but they aren't yet a collaborator. They want to go off into a corner and do their work and they usually don't work well at Intuit."*

Some of our chief executive interviewees noted the irony that, in the modern business era, progressive companies are becoming much more open about diversity and inclusion but much less liberal when it comes to tolerating dissent in the ranks. However, values are so crucial to the success of a business, particularly a new company that has set out its stall to be different, that illiberalism in the name of ethics is more than justifiable.

At Metro Bank, Craig Donaldson is a keen believer in FIFO (fit in or flip off is the polite version) and has shown the door to several recruits who have not been able to shake off old banking habits and embrace Metro's mission, culture and new sense of purpose.

> *"We've learned along the way because not many people have recently set up new banks in the UK, but we've been very clear about who we are and how we operate.*
>
> *"To begin with, we recruited people with banking experience, but part of our vision is to think like retailers whilst being the most professional bankers. In retail, the culture is that every customer who phones you or walks through the door is important, whereas in banking people are living off their legacy and we must never think like that because it's all about looking after customers.*
>
> *"We recruit against our values, with attitude being the key, and the people we recruit from outside banking are so much*

quicker to get it than people from banking. We've had to extend the induction for two weeks for people from other banks because we had to deconstruct them first so that they understand that Metro Bank is about creating a service and experience to delight fans. We don't have sales targets. Some people internally didn't believe that at first but it's a key part of our values."

At Lloyd's of London, meanwhile, Dame Inga Beale is fighting 329 years of conservatism and resistance to change as she tries to drag the insurance market into the twenty-first century. She once caused a revolt on the floor by daring to suggest on a hot summer Friday that underwriters might be allowed to remove their jackets and ties for just one day.

On another occasion, a syndicate asked if they could redesign their "box", as the desks in the market's great hall are called. Beale understood immediately the sensitivity of the request and allowed workmen to make the change in secret over an Easter weekend so that word did not leak out. But there was still uproar from diehards on Easter Tuesday when they saw the changes.

Like all purpose-driven leaders, Beale is possessed by a vision.

"Lloyd's is a bit antiquated, but it will be so great when it is modernised because it does fantastic things for society and it has got to where it is despite not modernising and despite some traditions that can get in the way.

"Some people go on about the old days but, once, Lloyd's had close to a 100% market share in the specialist sector of insurance. Now, it is closer to 8%. This is why we are tackling modernisation, so that we can compete in an ever more competitive world."

Despite this, she decided to back down on the two issues of dissent on the basis that there are going to be much bigger battles to fight and win. However, she will not budge on the core issues of inclusion, fairness and equality of opportunity.

 "A lot of what we do is making sure that people are being treated equally and don't feel disadvantaged because of the colour of their skin or their religion or things like that.

"At Lloyd's we still hear women referred to as 'box bitches' and 'box bunnies'. You wouldn't believe it, but it still happens. We're trying to eradicate that sort of thing, not tolerate it at all and make sure it's called out."

At Unipart, meanwhile, Carol Burke says a lot of work goes into maintaining the employee-owned company's strong culture as a lean manufacturer and progressive employer. The firm, which grew out of British Leyland's old car parts business, has developed a philosophy that it calls "The Unipart Way," supported by "the Unipart U" – one of the first company universities in Europe - to help employees develop their skills and advance.

"Our view is that people can achieve greatness if you give them the space, support and the opportunity to do that.

"Of course, what you then get are all the classic imperfections of human nature, so to achieve that in such an open environment is more difficult. You have to have discipline and you have to have standards and you have to do that in a way that keeps people engaged."

Burke adds that when there is a problem with an employee's performance, there are several options. For people who want to do a good job and find it difficult, the company offers training and coaching support. For people who, for whatever reason, do not want to make the effort to do a good job, the most likely step is separation. In both scenarios, she says Unipart seeks to treat individuals fairly and with respect for their dignity.

Create rituals to spread the message

The next level is to think about things you will establish, such as team meetings and regular supplier gatherings. Lego, for example, holds a worldwide "play day" every year, where all its office employees and factory employees put down their pens, pencils and machines and play for half a day. Says Judith Houston:

"The purpose is to remind everyone about what Lego does and how it does it. Lego is all about playing, it is all about encouraging the creativity in kids, but not just kids, also in everybody.

"Lego also has a stewardship agenda, denoting the historical meaning of being a guardian for kings. It's the whole concept of looking after what's entrusted to you and looking after it to the best of your ability for the children. That's the kind of tagline around stewardship, that everyone at Lego is a guardian of the brand."

Dame Inga Beale at Lloyd's adds:

"We spend a lot of time engaging with groups in the market. I spend an inordinate amount of time on that, listening, talking, explaining the strategy and my ideas and getting their feedback. We have a strategy for the market and the work we're doing on its modernisation affects more than 200 broking firms and every single managing agent here at Lloyd's. We've got to bring them on this journey.

"We could do it in a Big Bang, like the London Stock Exchange did. But we feel this essence of our negotiation and relationship-based market is so important that we don't want to destroy it, so we've somehow got to change it with the engagement of all the people around it. We spend so much time on winning their hearts and minds. We've already achieved two major changes that had never been done before."

This illustrates that the achievement of purpose requires fully committed leadership and widespread acceptance and the embracing of purpose at every level of the business. This embodies itself in practices, as well as public statements and messages on websites.

Senior leadership teams are usually very happy, indeed passionate about spreading the word. This is not ego or self-promotion but because they believe in the power of the good they are doing through their company. Chief executives and founders are interviewed often, but what is really insightful in purpose-led businesses is that employees on the shop floor are equally capable of explaining what the business does and why.

This is reflected by Richard Ellis, global director of corporate social responsibility at Walgreens Boots Alliance. He has seen how progressing from

CSR to a more broadly defined purpose has led to more people across businesses feel much more of a sense of ownership.

"In the early days, we were a bit of an oddity, almost on the corner of one of the floors. Nobody really understood what we did but we put a tick in the box, usually for the chairman, and occasionally we were dusted down if there was an invitation from a member of the royal family or a question from an NGO or a journalist. We were very much on the outside, looking in.

"Over the past 30 years, we've moved from the slipstream into the mainstream. Nowadays, CSR and purpose are very much the day-to-day work of the company, as opposed to something that was done 'over there'. I'm involved in all the key discussions with all the key decision makers. The agenda is centre stage."

A strong purpose-based corporate culture is the solution to many of the challenges of business. It manifests itself in self-motivated staff, natural innovation in ways of doing business and products, customer loyalty and mutually beneficial and supportive relationships with suppliers.

It is through a strong corporate culture that all these stakeholders see the benefit of creating, adopting and sustaining behaviours that embody a company's purpose. Purpose is the indispensable means to create such a corporate culture with the integrity necessary to maintain business success.

Burke at Unipart points out that the company focuses strongly on employee engagement as a route to competitive advantage. A culture in which employees are motivated to "go the extra mile" comes from employees taking a sense of pride in their role, feeling that the company is fair and caring, and from people being recognised for their effort and achievement in many different ways. Remuneration needs to be fair, but it is not the primary motivator for engagement.

Sir Mike Rake at BT adds:

"One of the big problems in the UK is that there is much less codetermination of the workforce than in mainland

Europe. A motivated workforce is a much more productive workforce. A workforce that's proud of the company it works for and believes that what it says is not just rhetoric is hugely powerful to getting the improvements we need in productivity, cooperation and codetermination.

"It's not just about having a tick in the box because your employees will see straight through that. They know when it is real and not real."

Creating a sense of understanding

To achieve an understanding of how to create the practices, you need to think through the following. Each company needs to determine how it will approach creating the sense and understanding of purpose with each of its own stakeholders. These may vary but, in essence, it is a simple set of questions.

Employees

How do you want your employees to commit around the purpose? Can you give them a sense of ownership and empowerment? Will the culture encourage ideas and suggestions on how you deliver your purpose?

Purposeful practice includes being honest with employees too. Will Butler-Adams at Brompton Bicycle, says:

"We're extraordinarily honest with our staff. Our staff know pretty much everything about the business. They know how much debt we have, how much cash we have in the bank and how much profit we make each month. We share our monthly management accounts and our departmental commentaries. I write a monthly report that goes to the board but pretty much all of it goes to the staff. We expect

our staff to know what's going on and, if they don't care about the company, they can push off because we need them to care.

"I changed the culture after I did the buyout. We've done some difficult things in the company – about seven years ago we got rid of piecework, which meant that a number of our staff had to take a pay cut. We said to our staff: 'Guys, this is not nice and it is unfair on you. But, unfortunately, if this business is going to survive for all of us, this is what we have to do'.

"If we stick to the truth and are fair, that seems to work for us. If your purpose and vision are strong enough and genuine, they will percolate through the business. They have to because they are in everything you do."

At The Eden Project, Sir Tim Smit also believes in building a sense that employees are valued contributors to an organisation.

"The thing that people want more than anything, I think, from me is they like to feel they are part of a very exciting gang. We have a great team and we throw great parties. I'd like to think we're kind and generous and that we look after our people. We have a sickness benefit scheme which is probably as good as you'll get anywhere in the world and very few abuse it. Because it's too precious to lose.

"Employees also like the fact that we have told them right from the start that we're going to make mistakes and that it's ok if they make some, too. Losing your fear of failure is the only way to grow and we find Eden people thrive on this liberation."

Customers

How do you communicate your purpose to customers? Can you engage them to the extent that they care equally about your purpose, building a preferential relationship and reputational enhancement?

Purpose is not a customer strategy – it's a promise to customers. This is a very important statement and that promise is around the values of the product or service, the qualities and the truth around the businesses.

Doug McMillon, president and chief executive of Wal-mart, said last year:

"Our customers care about their neighbours, their communities and the planet. They want to buy products that are good for the environment and the people who made them. They want items that are safe and healthy for their families. And, ultimately, they want to use their dollars, pounds or yen in a way that aligns with their values and has an impact on the world."

What is your Community?

How does your business define its "community" and then play a part in it that is aligned to your purpose, appropriate to it and helps to bolster employee and customer engagement?

At TOMS, the world-famous purpose-driven shoe company that gives one pair of shoes to people in developing countries for every pair sold in the West, Zita Cassizzi, TOMS' chief digital officer, believes there are five key action points for brands in search of a purposeful connection with consumers. These are: connect with your community, deliver content, products and services, build customer relationships for life, continue the conversation for life and create a culture of innovation.

Her list illustrates a sense of long-term thinking and a commitment to build relationships that go beyond the simple transactional norm.

Suppliers

How do you create a sense of mutual benefit, via your supplier and partnerships, that serve to provide greater depth and strength to the relationship and help serve your purpose and business?

In the aerospace industry, there have been well-publicised scandals alleging impropriety in supply relationships. Paul Kahn, president of Airbus Group in the UK, says:

"We put ethics at the heart of this organisation. You've got to have a culture that says: 'We're not going to do certain things.' That's about leadership and purpose. At Airbus, we've signed up to the United Nations Global Compact. That is discussed at a senior management level. Our strapline is 'We make it fly', so having the CSR and ethics compliance linked back to that becomes important."

Investors

How do you maintain relationships with investors based on them understanding your purpose, your culture and long-term aims, rather than short-term ones? What communication and examples will be used to illustrate the value of being purpose-driven?

Sally Tennant, chair of Duncan Lawrie Private Banking and investment analytics business Style Research, says companies with ethical credentials will find strong interest from investment firms with policies on responsible investing. She says:

"Embedding purpose in an organisation is a hard thing to do, but the rewards are there for investors who work on understanding it and taking a longer-term view."

Media

How do you establish good traditional and social media coverage based on authentic illustrations of how your purpose manifests itself? How can this activity bolster all relationships with other stakeholders and at the same time be a valuable engagement channel for new business and opportunities?

Lord Janvrin, now Senior Adviser to HSBC Private Bank (UK), says:

"I think there's always been a big premium on purpose and ethics, but there's no doubt that today the need to explain what you're doing in an open and honest way is hugely important."

Chapter summary

There are three key things for you to reflect upon in respect of your cultural ambition:

- **For you and your colleagues.** Your culture as it manifests itself through your personal behaviour will drive how your staff feel about you and the business. Done correctly, it creates loyalty, drives performance, fosters innovation and builds passionate commitment to what you are trying to do and the way you are delivering it through business.

- **For your world at large.** Your culture as it manifests itself through your practices with stakeholders represents the building block on which your wider reputation is based. It will also act as an illustration to others of what good business can be and its positive impact on the world.

- **For business stakeholders.** Your culture as it manifests itself through your people's behaviours will profoundly affect the way in which suppliers, investors and customers appreciate your business and why you do it in the way you do. It will build loyalty and longer-term relationships.

 Although the next chapter covers how you will unleash purpose within your people, at this point it will be useful to reflect on what you have read above and what you consider is important to the culture you want.

The onion model

First, we want to share with you a very useful model created by Professor Geert Hofstede that we use as the framework for some of our work in this area. He conducted what is possibly the largest assessment of how culture is crafted by values, both nationally and corporately, studying a large database of employees collected by IBM from 70 countries between 1967–73.

Many have followed the research with additional developments, but we share here his "onion" model as a simple graphic that can be interpreted easily for your own assessment.

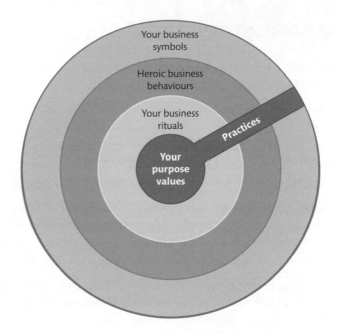

We like the onion because it is a simple way of analysing how various aspects of your practices create the culture.

The following exercise will allow you to ask yourself the questions necessary to create a vision and path to your desired state.

For each layer of the onion, peel back your own or your team's understanding of what is required and what is, perhaps, already in place.

- **Values:** this is at the core of your purpose and governance, how you behave and what you hold dear. List what values are intrinsic to you, your purpose and how you do business. These have to be non-negotiable and applicable across all stakeholder groups. The significance of placing these at the centre is that they should shape each other circle. For example, if your values didn't include respecting individuals or integrity, rituals might include inappropriate induction or reward mechanisms, something we witnessed in the banking sector. They will create heroes out of the wrong behaviours and fuel poor symbolism.

- **Rituals:** these help the group bond. They may consist of a weekly afternoon tea and catch-up, a way of celebrating success, in-group terminology or fun things that happen by routine. They shape behaviour within the office or workplace and act as touchstones for interaction with each other and the means through which communication works in all its forms. Don't just ask yourself about how often a newsletter goes out, or just the formal aspects, think less formally about what you do on special days. What will you do on people's birthdays, for example?

- **Heroes:** use this not as a means of championing individuals over others. Having a group of "favoured" individuals can prove destructive. Instead, what you want to identify is what will be recognised as heroic behaviour. What do you do when someone goes that extra mile to solve a difficult issue, or creates an amazing new innovation or, as in the case at Booth's Ilkley supermarket, an employee goes out of their way to check on the welfare of a customer who has been missed? These are heroic behaviours that allow all staff, potentially, to be recognised as a hero of the day.

- **Symbols:** the most significant symbol you will have in your business is actually the brand and how it is manifested actually helps motivate and support the culture. However, such symbols could also include the type of photographs you use on your material – the colour, particular language and graphics that have recognition elsewhere, that can affect perceptions of your own. For example, if you use pictures of items or scenes associated with an elite, expensive lifestyle, in various sectors it will lead to some people assuming that the business and its activities is not for them.

  If you prefer to evoke a sense of cheapness through how your brand manifests itself, it may encourage short cuts and a less valued attitude within other aspects of your operation.

- **Practices:** you will see that cutting across each ring is the practices that you will establish. These include your language, what time you set aside for certain activities and how you react to circumstances. A way to consider these is that they are the visual manifestation of your values set. It is fine to say that your values include a commitment to the environmental state of the planet. However, if you are seen to act in ways that show you to be wasteful or destructive, the culture will fail because the values are not manifested in your behaviour.

Creating purposeful practices will help foster an environment where you can work to unleash purpose within others in your organisation. This is what we call unleashing purpose in others and it is the sixth and final step to realising the purpose of your business.

Chapter 6

Inspire others

Introduction

There is an old African proverb that states:

"If you want to go fast, go alone.
If you want to go far, go together."

Highly motivated, purpose-powered businesses and their leaders may want, at times, to move fast in their purpose journey, but their task requires something other than long-distance vision, stamina and fortitude. Leaders can achieve little on their own.

Accomplishing their carefully crafted purpose necessitates the involvement of many colleagues, who all have their own personal situations and priorities. Suffice it to say that they will not have anywhere near as much passion and enthusiasm for the path ahead from that which resides in the leader. The motivations and rewards will always be different. But leaders need to find ways of engaging them, or otherwise their purpose will remain unfulfilled.

Simply put, they need to commit to unleashing in others the same purpose power that they have identified for themselves.

Are people drawn to you and your organisation because of what you stand for? Wouldn't it be so much more motivating for everyone if you knew that to be the case, rather than thinking people are with you simply for the money?

Imagine what your business would feel like if all your employees had joined you, based on having the same deep personal commitment to your business purpose as you do. It would feel more energised, more committed, happier, more focused and, undoubtedly, more productive.

Being clear about your personal and business purpose, alongside the values both defined within the business, will attract the type of people who will be capable of feeling equally passionate about your purpose-powered business.

The purpose of the business tells people what they can join in, what they can contribute to, what they can feel in terms of making a significant contribution and it needs to be amplified by your commitment to that purpose. You should be able to say: "This is what we are about, this is how we will do it and you can decide if it is what you want to spend your time on."

By others, we are not referring only to your team's potential. It's also about your suppliers, investors, customers and other stakeholders. As raving fans, they can help promote your business, champion it and help it grow. So how do you get them to be even half as committed to the idea of your business's purpose as you are?

Encourage team togetherness

The purpose movement is only now becoming recognised as a mainstream business movement and there are still dozens of different views and voices about the principles or formula to get it right. The difficulty is that, when it comes to motivating teams around purpose, getting too hung up on formula and process is absolutely the wrong thing to do.

When Sir Tim Smit talks about his "gang", you can tell he is talking in an emotional rather than rational sense. The same can be said of Edwin Booth when he talks of his family within the business and means more than just those with his surname.

When one enters the head office of Paperchase, positioned over the top of its flagship store in Central London, everything about the environment, the smiles on people's faces, the clutter of design and palpable energy of CEO Timothy Melgund and his team illustrates the purpose of putting fun into functionality.

Everything exudes the high qualities of the product ranges, the unique designs, but with a belief that they are making life that little bit more colourful. They take the mundane, say a stapler machine, and turn it into something worthy of becoming a treasured item or a sought-after gift. They enrich the world by creating vibrancy and excitement in stationery that simply wouldn't occur if they lacked such sense of purpose.

Says Melgund:

> *"The way I look at it is that you're either a Paperchase person or you're not and it's terribly important to make sure that everyone we employ, whether in our stores or the head office, is a Paperchase person. If they're not, they're not going to feel particularly comfortable and they're not going to give of their best.*

"If they don't feel part of the overall team and don't have the same life values, it's going to be difficult for the team you're putting them into and difficult for the person you put into the team. It's like buying a house, as soon as you cross the threshold, you know within seconds whether you're going to fit in."

Create a movement

You won't see many weighty tomes on mass mobilisation or turning corporate agendas into movements. This tends to be something learned over time through experience. But the brands that develop followings through a purpose-led agenda have a head start.

At Patagonia, Ryan Gellert says:

"We average close to 1,000 applicants for every vacancy that we have. We have people who know the brand and are very excited to join. There's a difference between saying that things are important and investing your time and resources in them.

"Different companies have different levels of commitment but we're committed to continuing to move the goalposts back and challenge ourselves on what it means to be a company that not only can exist but should exist 100 years from now."

Jay Coen Gilbert is endeavouring to generate the same attitude at B Corporation.

"It started for us at AND 1 around people that worked in our footwear and clothing factories and their extended families. Now at B Lab, through the community of more than 2,000 B Corporations, we're effectively making a meaningful platform cool. It's been a journey but over three to five years it became clear that we could envision a platform that was set up exclusively and powerfully to create meaning and purpose and a positive impact in the world."

Stephen Greene is cofounder of RockCorps, a pro-social American production company that uses music to inspire people to volunteer and get involved in their communities, working as a partner to major brands. Since the firm was set up in 2005, it has attracted more than 170,000 volunteers who have given more than 700,000 hours to 2,500 global charities.

> *"Our belief then – and the world has really caught up with this – was that brands want to communicate who they are around community and give something back. We've seen a real change over the last 12 years. If we can prove that by doing these types of programmes, we can impact brands' bottom lines and shareholder returns, now we're cooking with gas and can really look at societal change."*

The key to unleashing purpose in others in order to drive performance in the business needs to be a combination of the rational and the emotional. But, unlike conventional business, the winning recipe requires rational requirements to be put in place simply to create the sense of comfort that the more emotional need to flourish.

Accommodate the rational

Put in place the rational needs of your team members, such as a safe working environment, appropriate remuneration and the necessary equipment. Such comfort factors are the entry point to bring your people into a state of mind where they are not burdened by being overly concerned for those rational needs.

The culture-defining practices we covered in the last chapter will also be sound foundations upon which to let loose the power of emotion.

Embrace the emotional

We are emotional beasts and it is emotion that allows us to drive purposefulness in others. Emotions are how people really give of themselves, so inspiring people to embrace your business's purpose and their own sense of personal fulfilment and achievement will help give them an immense sense of the opportunity your business offers.

Such fulfilment comes from creating a combination of feeling one is contributing something and that the contribution is being appreciated. It is therefore something that needs to be a collective experience.

If we can create the right emotion, energy, creativity, fun and passion, we can mobilise people to commit heart and soul to it.

We all know business leaders who speak with high levels of gravitas, citing a corporate mission and a set of values and waving purpose statements and motivational posters, but too often they are actually bland individuals lacking emotion and unable to attract followers.

They may have engaged a major professional firm to draw up such statements, undertaken extensive consultation and used focus groups. But no one believes any of it because the boss clearly doesn't have an emotional stake in it.

To get purpose into others, get passionate. And to get passionate about purpose, get emotional. As the late Body Shop founder Anita Roddick put it:

"We communicate with passion, and passion persuades."

Dame Stephanie Shirley, known famously as Stevie, founded early computer software firm Freelance Programmers in 1962. A remarkable female pioneer of her time, who as a child fled Nazi Germany, she built up a multi-million digital business and then determined to give her wealth away, supporting many causes but in particular women's rights and autism.

Speaking at a One Hundred "Knot" network event, she not only described the challenges around a woman creating a purpose-driven business but also how she then set up a foundation in 1986 to give away more than £67m of her personal wealth.

"I did it because of my personal history. I needed to justify the fact that my life was saved."

She also suffered personal tragedy when her late son Giles became profoundly autistic at the age of two, permanently losing the ability to speak.

"If success were easy, we'd all be millionaires and in my case it came in the midst of family tragedy and crisis."

Giles died at the age of 35 but Dame Stephanie is clear in her mindset:

"I've now learned to live without Giles and his need of me. I've tried to use our family's terrible experiences for good by investing most of my wealth, and all of my time really, in

autism care, education and research. Philanthropy not only gives great joy and intellectual fulfilment; it's one of the few ways to enjoy losing everything."

Annabel Karmel's own emotional entrance into the baby foods market gives her immediate resonance with customers, employees and parents who can only imagine what she went through.

"The purpose and passion started as a legacy for Natasha and continued as a passion for other children to live longer. It's a passion that permeates into the company's products. Everything we do is for the benefit of children. Take baby food. It's in the dark ages, the only section of the supermarket that's totally ambient and long-life. It's not fresh or frozen so the child is often actually eating food older than themselves.

"I introduced fresh, chilled baby food, but there's no electricity in supermarket baby aisles. You can't put fresh, chilled baby food there. You have to put it in a totally separate area of the supermarket where mothers don't go. We ended up with high wastage and had to withdraw it. But from that experience, we have ended up with a very high-quality range of ambient baby food that has done very well and a successful range of frozen baby food in Australia. I don't think I would have done that any other way. The opposite of success isn't failure, it's not trying."

 Don't be shy of showing emotion yourself, for your purpose and all it means to you. Be prepared to talk to anyone and everyone about what you do and your business. Be keen to have those around you exceed your own ambition, cleverness and skills. And be ambitious for your purpose and people. Your aim is to create passionate advocates for your business, your services, products, how you do things and in so doing create a good business doing good. You want to attract talent and then retain it and keep everyone inspired on the purpose journey.

Inspire belief

A purposeful leader alone cannot make the business a purpose business unless they can ignite such passion in everyone else. It is also clear that an individual cannot ignite purpose in others unless they have done so within themselves.

Any successful sales person will relate that the key is believing in the product and the benefits it will genuinely confer on a purchaser. Purpose-led businesses foster that level of belief in everyone with whom they come into contact. Their sense of authenticity permeates all aspects of their business relationships, from suppliers, investors, distributors and customers.

At TSB Bank, Paul Pester says:

> *"There's no one thing you can do to change the hearts and minds of the employees. When we set up the bank in 2011, there were five of us. Now there are more than 8,000. Filling those employees with a sense of purpose and direction has been one of the key areas of focus for me.*
>
> *"Purpose is a business strategy for us. It's a crystal-clear strategy for TSB to differentiate itself by getting back to the core purpose of a bank. We've grown deposits by 46% since January 2014. Now we're the most recommended high street bank in the UK. Why has all that happened? The strategy is part of it but the way we have engaged our partners has been absolutely vital."*

A fundamental undeniable human truth is that we all have a desire to belong. A true sense of belonging occurs only when we are surrounded by those who feel the same about things, care about what we care for and approach life on the basis of a similar values set.

We are essentially tribal and those who work in leading companies feel themselves part of some bigger belonging. The unifying "common bonds" are now about a way of thinking, creativity or a lifestyle approach rather than race, religion or traditional culture.

Unleash your passion for business

The energy you require to lead purposefully comes from an innate passion to do whatever your stated purpose is. Running a business of any kind requires determination, perseverance and dogged determination, but to lead a purposeful team and business takes enormous passion.

Think about just how passionate you are about your business. Only each individual truly knows whether spending 18 hours doing something that they really care about is fun or not. If what you were passionate about was a football team, or art or cycling say, it would be described simply as your passion. It's less common with business but, if you are leading a purposeful company, there should be an expectation that it is your passion and that you will exude it in all you say and do.

Sharing your purpose vision

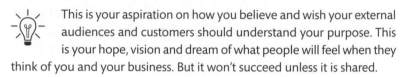 This is your aspiration on how you believe and wish your external audiences and customers should understand your purpose. This is your hope, vision and dream of what people will feel when they think of you and your business. But it won't succeed unless it is shared.

Purposeful leaders know how to talk, when to talk and how to get others to talk to them. They learn to have the right conversations at the right times in order to progress their agenda.

The following conversations are ones you should consider having with suppliers, employees, investors, customers and other key stakeholders.

1. **The vision conversation:** sharing your ambition and vision around the business and its purpose. Aim to create a powerful energising sense of ambition, which is big enough to inspire and require people to look at you and your business as different and feel energised to accept change and motivated to help bring it about.

2. **The valued relationship conversation:** genuinely engaging individuals by showing trust and confidence in them as partners in your ambition. Be open and honest and, if necessary, address challenging issues, but have conversations where people feel valued and appreciated.

3. **The success conversation:** an essential component in making people understand what you define as success, how it will manifest itself and how you will celebrate it. It will be goal-based but this conversation must be an emotional one. It's about creating the sense of a goal being possible and recognisable, and not about listing sales targets.

4. **The freedom conversation:** encouraging your team, suppliers and other stakeholders to set aside traditional parameters of

responsibility, and empowering them to think much wider, using their experience, expertise and enthusiasm to create new ideas, options and solutions.

5. **The collaborative conversation:** bringing people on side in a specific collaborative way, identifying mutual benefits from closer association. This might include trading expertise or resources in kind, co-hosting events or acting as referral partners, recommending clients. Whatever the opportunity, such conversations can reap often unexpected and highly valuable rewards, so long as they remain wedded to your business purpose.

Authentic leadership

A person with purpose is a leader. A leader can lead only if they have those who will follow. The facts are that you cannot unleash purpose in others unless you can lead. There is nothing more vital to the process of this activation than your leadership. These are the traits that give you the necessary ability to motivate and lead yourself and others around your business. The skill and habit of authentic leadership and motivation is your foundation to instil confidence in others and breathe life into your dreams.

As Dame Julia Cleverdon, former CEO of Business in the Community, says:

> *"Leaders are like tea bags. You only know how strong they are when they get in hot water."*

 Ben Fletcher, former MD, has a story about his promotion to the top job that shows his questioning style and conviction that leaders need to ask uncomfortable questions.

> *"One of the first questions I asked at board meetings was what was the point of the company.*
>
> *"Actually, a lot of the responses were about values, about caring. And there was a lot of rich and good things going on. However, there wasn't necessarily a single unifying purpose position which everyone could express. The way I*

tried to articulate this was that we're doing loads of good work but we now need to know why we're doing it. Being better able to understand our role in the industry, we can be confident and look forward and all the work we're going to do is right and that it all adds together to a whole."

Alex Mahon, former chief executive of Shine Group, now CEO of design and visual effects software firm The Foundry, says:

"The concept of having a purpose for the business is critical because it provides clarity and a galvanisation around a theme that people in the business want to be part of.

"Laying it out doesn't solve everything but it's incredibly useful for clarifying what you believe you stand for as a group of individuals and where people fit with that. And then using that to set how you should work within it, what your style is and how you should approach things.

"At Shine we had a template saying that we wanted to inspire, create and shine. We were very clear that our mission was creating outstanding hits that delight and inspire audiences around the world. Then we had a very clear set of behaviours that went with that so everybody in the company knew what we were here to do. Once you roll it out properly and put it through people's assessments and how you judge yourself as a company, it can be all-pervasive."

For Sir Mike Rake at BT, meanwhile, leadership means inspiring employees around a common vision.

"When I arrived at BT, pride in what we did was only cited by 30% of the workforce. Now it is up around 60–70%. A lot of volunteering was going on, almost in spite of the organisation. People just wanted to do it for their communities. As we made it easier and gave leadership on the subject, we got more enthusiasm.

"Our purpose at BT is to use technology to improve the state of the world. We facilitate communication, which does

improve the state of the world through education, increased productivity, healthcare and many other things. Given leadership, our people have really bought that."

Troubleshooting

Whatever the purpose that's under development, problems will essentially be similar. How you deal with such difficulties and offer those involved the necessary leadership to get beyond them will depend on what we can term "enlightened leadership". This is a combination of characteristics:

- The ability to learn to dominate the events that surround you.

- The ability not to allow anything to divert you from the purpose.

- Being prepared to accept full responsibility.

- Endeavouring to inspire confidence in others.

Brandpie cofounder Dave Allen says he first saw the power of purpose in the early 1990s when he was working on the Castrol brand, which had been neglected and regarded simply as a "cash cow".

> *"We focused back in on the core purpose of Castrol, which way back had a phrase called 'liquid engineering'. That phrase had gone out of favour, but we got them to focus back on premium quality and technology-led high performance.*

> *"Within two years, they were getting four more margin points out of the Castrol brand and focusing massively on it. It was the power of what was right under their nose, and reminding everyone there that Castrol was liquid engineering, that really motivated Castrol's people as well. They were all passionate about the Castrol brand and, by making it look like a world leader, all these things fitted together. You got a more engaged workforce and just saw the business start to fly."*

At Notonthehighstreet.com, Simon Belsham says the focus on the online marketplace's 5,000 creative business partners and their customers made him question a practice of selling branded goods that the company had got into before he joined.

> *"We were selling product that didn't meet our purpose. They were branded products that were supplied by bigger businesses that you could find anywhere. We talked about being a curated marketplace and what Notonthehighstreet.com really stood for."*

Belsham decided to create guidelines governing what products the company sold on its marketplace and worked with partners over six months to remove many branded products from its site.

> *"Our sales went backwards, but it was critical that we got back to our purpose. You have to stand for something. Otherwise, why will people go there? What makes us different are unique quality products from the best small creative businesses and, if we were selling products that didn't meet that, we had to stop it."*

John Fallon at Pearson tells of a similar experience when the company's academic testing operations fell short of its commitment to accountability of standards.

> *"Students in Texas were taking 12 or more different tests before they could graduate from high school. In my view, in hindsight, we should have been more accountable in saying to our partner that this was too many tests and we should be focusing on fewer, better, smarter assessments that were not quite as onerous. We didn't do that soon enough and, as a result, there was a big political controversy, which played a part in us losing the testing contract. If you don't hold yourself accountable and build accountability into everything you do, it's actually not in the long-term interests of the business."*

 Passionate, purpose-driven creative people turn visions into realities. They do so with the ability to lead others and themselves on the necessary course to success. Leadership capability is what makes the pursuit of such ideas sustainable, scaleable and, ultimately, successful. To grow and sustain idea activation, you must be able to keep others fully engaged with your ideas.

Action-centred, purpose-focused leadership

Purposeful leadership is about the projection of your personality and character. The leadership of a purpose as an idea is complemented by the projection of the aspiration and its own character. As such, the whole process of projecting the purpose and your leadership role with it is, by nature, personal.

You will embody the character of the idea as it will, inevitably, embody your own as its creator. This means that, if your personality and personal leadership traits are to lead with a light touch, with a sense of humour, style and a spirit of adventure, then the idea will advance in the same manner. It is your personality that is embodied in the purpose and that will inspire in others confidence, respect, mutual affection and a love of the vision.

The light touch should be underpinned by a tight grip on the purpose and its focus, not without difficulty sometimes to pull off successfully, but essential if you are going to succeed.

Learn leadership from the experts

John Adair is a British academic and business guru who is a world-renowned leadership theorist and author of 40 books on business, military and other leadership. He is a former Army officer and was previously senior lecturer at The Royal Military Academy Sandhurst.

Over a million managers have gone through his action-centred training courses, which reflect the military approach to leadership. His principles can be helpful in purpose activation. There are three broad approaches to the understanding of leadership, which any purpose activator should appreciate:

- **Qualities:** what you are, what you embody and how you behave – what we have covered in you finding your own purpose.

- **Situational:** what you know about the environment within which you operate.

- **Functional:** what you do in terms of your role and function and how the business operates.

 These blend together to create the rounded leadership personality and character that you will embody through your purpose-driven development.

Adair's Action-Centered Leadership (ACL) model was first published in 1973, highlighting the key actions that leaders have to take when managing their teams. It groups these responsibilities together under three key areas:

- **Task:** achieving the team's goal.

- **Team:** developing and building your team, so that it's ever more effective.

- **Individual:** helping individuals develop their full potential in the workplace.

These areas are represented by three interlocking circles.

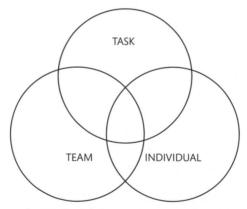

Three circles model © John Adair

In our view, purpose can sit at the heart of the cross-over of these three circles. In terms of the Task, good leaders will invariably see the "why", the purpose, in that area. We would also suggest that the "why" becomes paramount to engaging and motivating stakeholders, the Team, whilst for the individual, such clarity of purpose is the driving force to maintain commitment.

Purpose leader

Getting this right means that in our view purpose sits wholeheartedly at the centre of the ACL model. Leaders must balance the actions they take across all three areas if they want their group to succeed. The areas are interdependent. If a leader focuses too much on one area and neglects the other two, then the group will experience problems.

Although the diagram shows all the circles as being the same size, this doesn't mean that leaders should always divide up their effort across these areas equally. Rather, the appropriate balance varies according to the situation and, over time, these may well change.

In unleashing purpose in others, you will need to keep the task of the business at the fore, but the individual needs of the people you are engaging will need to be prioritised and addressed while team or stakeholders relationships will require constant attention and management. The following are the specific functions you will be expected to undertake:

1. **Leading the business direction:** for the business overall, you will know exactly where it is heading, with your vision and a clarity of purpose.

2. **Leading the decision making:** making the strategic and important policy decisions, encompassing both the responsibility for things when they might go wrong.

3. **Leading the means of making it happen:** this is the practical function of strategic leadership, managing what is happening, monitoring target progress and reviewing performance against the agreed plan.

4. **Leading organisation and structure:** managing the relationship between the various individuals or teams and relationships, which are part of your activation plan.

5. **Leading the corporate culture:** encouraging and enthusing people and instilling the enthusiasm and passion for the idea within your people, building excellent team spirit and high morale.

6. **Leading external relationships:** building relationships and cooperation with project allies, external partners and other organisations critical to the ideas development.

There are also generic qualities, including enthusiasm, integrity, moral courage, fairness, warmth and humility that are necessary for a purpose activator to become successful and recognised as a leader who instils confidence in others. An enthusiastic person tends to inspire enthusiasm in others.

Empower purpose-powered practices

You as a leader have the power, influence and ability to make things happen, to instigate processes, arrange resources, hold meetings, and so on. However, that is not how you create purpose-powered practices and in so doing inspire others.

To unleash this, you need to empower everyone in the business regardless of any hierarchy, to allow them to take responsibility for the purpose. You need to empower individuals themselves to build their empowered workplaces. This should make you think differently about the type of practices your business will be operating with, which manifest the type of purpose business you want. These practices will support the recognition and the performance aspects of the business.

Start with giving everyone a voice and allowing them to interface across boundaries, teams, roles and any other potentially dividing lines. Introduce recognitions of contribution and achievement, celebrate success, have a weekly hero and create a sense of achievement, trust, ambition and passion.

Taking all the above into practice means completing the following:

1. **Whatever you practise bcomes the practice of others.** This gives you the ability to influence everything but it also has one major risk: it means that you yourself must never let that sense of purpose lapse. Your approach – your illustration of the values you wish to see embodied – are essential in creating that culture and inspiring others. You must be clear with your messaging. Be consistent with your attitudes. Be alert to what is happening elsewhere that influences your purpose.

   There is no room in this game for the statement "Do as the preacher says and not as he does." It is all about your actions.

2. **Identify your fellow champions.** Within any business from an employee base of one or when taking over thousands, work quickly to identify your purpose champions who get the purpose and are excited about being internal as well as external advocates for your purpose.

These are your allies in the creation of your culture. They will be there when you aren't. They will be helping to create the conscious practices to embed your agenda. When possible, form them into a mutually supportive team and, before long, you will see that your team is keeping you on the purpose track rather than the other way around.

3. **Express purpose beyond any constraints of your business:** This can appear a challenge but it really means understanding what issues are relevant to your business purpose and don't feel constrained by normal practices to ignore them.

Ben Fletcher realised that the defective eyesight of hundreds of thousands of children was affecting literacy levels and educational attainment and decided to do something about it. Although children often are viewed by optician businesses as expensive to service and generating low returns, Fletcher saw a direct correlation between that social issue and how his business could help, creating a partnership with the National Literacy Trust to address the matter.

Fletcher says of the purpose conversations that preceded this and other initiatives:

> *"Our first rigorous setting of our strategic choices was: Does it help advance the purpose? Then: Does it help power the purpose forward? Does it make money, is it investible? And all the rest of it. Actually, those are irrelevant if something doesn't help us be the organisation we want to be."*

In the case of the National Literacy Trust scheme, it had the effect of parents of children seeing Boots as the optician of choice, with a boost of customer loyalty, recognition and reputation. It wasn't Fletcher's motivation but it was a pleasing business result for doing good.

4. **Foster open channels of communication:** Don't fall into the trap of so many companies and a top-down communication from culture. You want a team that has confidence in communicating up, down and sideways about how they feel generally and, importantly, how the purpose is helping performance, shaping activities, and so forth.

 As a leader, you may have the clear purpose and direction in your mind, but you should see as a vital asset an engaged group of employees who transmit as well as receive. Give your people both structured and ad-hoc ways to make their ideas, thoughts, feelings and observations known. You want them to know that their contributions, however challenging, are a valued part of the purpose culture.

5. **Build the means to show appreciation:** Your purpose-driven employees don't just work because of the money and, therefore, money is a flat, dull method of simply recognising time rather than performance. Those who have embraced the purpose not only give more, but, to be fair to them, often require a different type of reward mechanism than simply financial stability.

Often, they are driven by a desire for group or peer recognition, a need to feel that the senior leadership appreciates their contribution. The best ways can be small or large, a handwritten postcard of thanks on someone's desk or a surprise "party" and cake in the office, or an extra day's leave with a fun trip thrown in.

Whatever is appropriate for your culture, the means to thank is a key component of creating a purpose-driven workplace.

Chapter summary

Purpose-driven leadership is about putting purpose at the centre of building an organisation's leadership and delivery capacity. It is a positive, constructive leadership model that challenges an organisation to clearly focus on defining its purpose, by way of creating a robust integrity around decision making, the encouragement of its people and the corporate character.

Remember the importance of leadership in motivating your team members and encouraging them to exceed their expectations. By taking steps to become a transformational leader, you can encourage loyalty and trust and inspire, support and recognise others. More than this, you can inspire them to achieve extraordinary things.

In unleashing purpose in others, consider the following:

- **What you want from people.** Be clear about the level of commitment you require. Be prepared to hold a variety of conversations across all stakeholders. Be clear on the values that will drive your business. Be clear on your own practices.

- **What the world will expect from you all.** Be clear on what the world expects from the position you have taken. Understand how your people interface and represent you. Ensure the corporate behaviours are in synergy with social expectations.

- **What people want from you.** Be sure of what people expect from you. Be sure to live up to those expectations. Establish the practices that empower. Create ease of communication. Build a basis of the rational needs.

The six steps are now complete. The next chapter circles around the purpose agenda and brings together such thinking in a guide to live purposefully and the basis on which it must be lived, namely authenticity.

Chapter 7

Live life and prosper

Introduction

If the purpose you wish to create is worthwhile and you believe sufficiently in it to commit your time and energy to create it, then you will want, above all, to be successful. You will put your purpose and business idea ahead of other considerations. You will make sacrifices as you would if you were nurturing a child.

This is where, for some people, there is a risk that the purpose becomes so all-encompassing that they will cut corners, take shortcuts or compromise on their values and integrity. To do so is to take the path to failure.

When you start declaring to the world that you have a great new purpose for yourself or the business that it should embrace, you have to do so from the most solid of personal foundations. These will be based on an appropriate and honest way to behave to others, and in this you will need to be as sure of yourself as much as you are in your purpose.

This is where your moral compass and set of values and characteristics need to exist authentically and, in so doing, they will, inevitably, coexist within your purpose idea and the dealings you have on its behalf.

If you wish to promote a purpose with a particular quality, you must make sure that quality is really there in yourself. If you are going to promote a new caring business, then you must yourself be caring. If you are offering an innovative alternative to an existing product, you must be equally innovative in your thinking. The authentic connection between you, your purpose and those you wish to engage is crucial. The key point is that it cannot be faked – it must be authentic.

Given that your purpose must emerge from your thinking, there should be little difficulty in establishing authenticity. You simply cannot create really great purpose unless some of you and what you believe is mixed into it.

What each of us creates may impact on different people in different ways, but, ultimately, for a purposeful business to prosper, it must carry what you believe in. If it stands a chance of being successful, it has to have an integrity and authenticity, which engages people and lasts. Without that, however good the communication and products are, they will be unlikely to achieve the full potential you had in mind.

Could anyone argue that Apple cofounder Steve Jobs didn't believe and put himself into his product, or that Sir Richard Branson's core values don't permeate the Virgin brand? The simple appreciation is that true purpose-driven business leaders are not simply doing a job – they are expressing themselves and sharing their thinking with the world. This is authentic purpose, based on authentic values.

Sometimes, challenges will arise from dramatic experiences, backgrounds or other factors. Sir Richard famously said in his autobiography *Losing my Virginity* that the night he spent in Dover Prison after being arrested as part of a VAT investigation to do with records he was importing from Europe, was a seminal event for him, culminating in a strict pledge to himself never to do anything unethical in his business.

"There have been times when I could have succumbed to some form of bribe, or could have had my way by offering one. But ever since that night in Dover Prison I have never been tempted to break my vow. My parents always drummed into me that all you have in life is your reputation: you may be very rich, but if you lose your good name you'll never be happy."

Achieving authenticity

Authenticity was defined years ago by psychologist Brian Goldman as "the unimpeded operation of one's true or core self in one's daily enterprise". This is an inspiring idea in its own right. An aspiration that one would surely want for everyone in the world, however unrealistic that thought is. The belief, or indeed ambition, that everyone can undertake day-to-day work without compromise, fear or favour, based upon what they believe in and know they enjoy and are good at is a wonderful idea.

To achieve this requires self-knowledge and self-awareness, an appreciation of what the inner you really enjoys in life and what you believe. Authentic people accept their strengths and weaknesses. They are accountable. They are connected to their values and desires and act deliberately in ways that are consistent with those qualities.

If you bring such authenticity to a good idea, it will be injected with a set of rare qualities, which will shine through, be obvious to people and result in their engagement. So how does one assess one's own authenticity?

Authentic self-awareness

Authenticity starts when you either consciously set out to be genuine or simply always have been. If the latter is true, it is still worthwhile considering the awareness you have of what that looks and feels like, and that you have committed to act in accordance with your genuine nature, even when it is difficult. This is where you assess how you would behave when no one is looking.

When you understand and then live with this kind of self-awareness, your decisions become easier because you are not diverted by the shady or unethical, but are free to choose things that move you closer to your idea creation by the same set of values by which you live. You can easily turn your back on disreputable suppliers, unethical partners, cheap or dangerous conditions. Even if they mean short-term delay or inconvenience, the alternatives will lead to longer-term security and success.

Sir Mike Rake of BT says:

> *"Your decisions become easier when you act with purpose and so do those of your employees. Look at what happened in the banking crisis. During the boom times, the culture became aggressive. People didn't necessarily think they were doing anything wrong and life is not always black and white. It's often grey and there are difficult balances to be struck.*
>
> *"With the bank mis-selling, you have to remember that it is quite normal in the capitalist system to incentivise people to sell. But doing it fairly and openly in the proper way is the right thing to do.*
>
> *"If someone is self-employed, for example, banks shouldn't have sold personal protection insurance to them. But if you have the right purpose, doing that wouldn't even have occurred to bank staff because their compass would always take them away from it. Common sense would have told them it wasn't the right thing to do."*

Being authentic may make you or some decisions you make unpopular but, in the end, it allows you to live a more open, honest and fulfilling life. The culmination of this somewhat intangible sense of authenticity can be turned through such actions and decisions into tangible outcomes.

Being authentic makes you feel better. You will be more optimistic and resilient. You will retain a focus on the purpose behind your idea-related decisions and be more likely to be able to follow through on your goals.

Realising your authenticity

Here are three simple tips on determining your own authentic approach:

- **Be sure about what you believe in.** It's hard to behave in an authentic way if you do not know what you truly believe in. Be sure you understand what feels right to you and understand how your actions align to this thinking. If you are certain what you care about, then authenticity simply will become a part of you.

- **Approach with an open mind.** You will develop and grow personally and your authenticity flourishes when you are capable of understanding the world from every perspective. A closed mind traps you and your purpose. Challenge yourself to be open to new experiences, which will enhance your authentic appreciation of others and the world at large.

- **Notice when you are being untrue.** You need to pay particular attention to those times when you are insincere in your thoughts, words and speech or, indeed, if you act in a way that doesn't align with your values. Understand why. Were you trying to save embarrassment, time or money? Understand what triggered this and then create your own techniques to stop it happening again.

Authenticity and self-promotion

At this point, something needs to be said about an aspect of purpose activation that is of ever-growing importance: the role of self-promotion alongside the promotion of the purpose.

Over the last 20 years we have seen a change in society where across all roles, sectors and specialisms there has been a cultural shift towards self-promotion as the means through which to achieve success.

The rise of social media platforms and reality TV has meant that we all expect people who are destined to be successful in their objectives to almost conform to a multi-marketing-driven plan of promotion. This is something that many people in previous generations would not have been comfortable with.

It may still feel terribly uncomfortable to front up, take the stage and deal with the resulting attention. However, in order to activate your purpose effectively and ensure the authenticity of your leadership and its justified reward, this modest and more traditional British approach is now dead.

To many, there will appear something about self-marketing that sounds, or at least seems, inherently uncomfortable, immodest or fake. This can, therefore, look like a risk and challenge to authentic messaging.

However, it needs to be looked at in another way. The most successful self-marketing is not created as some sort of deceitful campaign to acquire glory or some other reward. Rather, it is an ongoing aspect of the development of individuals and their purpose and business and should stem from an authentic need to get business awareness out to the world.

Instead of this becoming a risky and delusional self-promotional ego trip, the best self-marketing will build knowledge of what you have done and think and respect for what you and your business are trying to achieve. A good self-marketing strategy should start with the intrinsic and authentic values and interests that relate to your track record and skills relative to the idea activation.

You can highlight roles you have played, previous ideas that you have created and reflect your own personal characteristics and values. These will demonstrate your strengths and people will respect you for something that they can see you have really done.

Essentially, you need to illustrate to the world a portfolio that embraces your characteristics as well as your past works. Determine which platforms you wish to use but your own web presence on social media sites such as Twitter, LinkedIn and Facebook should become aligned to best presenting you, your history, what you think and what you aspire to achieve with your idea.

Our personal histories

True authenticity is highly personal. For John, it started in the Army 30 years ago, as it was there that he was first truly immersed in the day-to-day activities he loved. Although it wasn't always comfortable, and being cold, wet, tired, hungry and sometimes in intense danger went with the job, he was living with fellow soldiers and officers by a unifying and immensely strong set of values.

These remain and are not some sort of general values stated in corporate value statements, but a collection of ideals and virtues that are important to John individually and also his collective group from that period. These values made them proud of what they did, how they did it and who they did it with.

> *"Occasionally, something didn't conform to those values and, when that happened, we all knew we had failed the wider team and ourselves. It was then that we would work to ensure it didn't happen again."*

This awareness takes work to determine what we find true and authentic in our lives and roles, but it is worthwhile because it teaches us something about ourselves that we might never previously have appreciated.

One part of John's authentic self-assessment is that he realises that, although he has consistently created value in people, in projects and their financing, at each stage his ambition to have an impact has never quite been satisfied.

> *"There is in the world a never-ending need to care for the vulnerable in the world and the vulnerability of the world itself."*

Where and how does one address such need? We all have to make our own decisions on that, whether it is a local need or an issue on the other side of the planet. Whatever set of choices one makes, none of us wishes to be anything less than the most affective at trying to make into a reality the change we want to see in the world a reality.

John knows that this is his authentic ambition and believes his purpose of helping people maximise their potential is the means through which he will play his part.

For Andrew, there is a similar task of setting achievable goals when what motivates him in life is constantly to find new truths that are not known, to demonstrate that many perceived truths are not true at all and to reveal facts, thinking and ideas that could and should make a difference to people's lives.

It is easy to see where such ambition begins by questioning the world around oneself, but where does it end? Again, that's a set of individual decisions that can be known only when situations present themselves and choices have to be made.

He is not a war reporter or a crusader for justice who puts his life on the line in his work, though he deeply respects those who do. But truth is uncomfortable sometimes and so can be some of its consequences. How far does one wander in search of it?

You will each have your own stories and challenges. Commercial, social and environmental entrepreneurs are best served when they build legitimacy around a solid purpose for ideas and approaches based upon their own authentic values.

It can take an enormous amount of energy to persuade others that your business will transform the world as they know it. These purpose leaders must also find ways to gain access and influence political, corporate and thought leaders who will embrace their idea to then leverage other connections to drive wider implementation. The authentic foundation is what each purpose powered leader should strive towards.

Your life story

Your purposeful life is just that. It is your life and your story. So when you consider writing your life story, perhaps albeit in your own mind only, why would you not make it the most meaningful and purposeful you could?

After all, as the hero of your own story, you wouldn't want to be anything less than the best you can be.

Some people wrongly suggest that being able to achieve that sense of purpose creates an ultimately effortless living because they equate it to the saying that, if you work at what you enjoy, you will never work a day in your life. That isn't true.

Certainly, in one regard, when you have purpose, you can become so certain of what you are trying to achieve and your personal sense of direction that you can alleviate a lot of stress from yourself, make difficult decisions more easily and navigate some of life's challenges. You can feel greater certainty about your life and have the confidence to trust in yourself making progress against your goals.

However, with great purpose comes great responsibility and for all the advantages that the above sentiments provide, the day-to-day challenges of business, economic issues, health, relationships, even the weather, can still be troublesome. Clarity of purpose certainly doesn't make life or running a business effortless. It simply makes it better.

Leading purposefully brings with it, therefore, great benefit and what should be a greater sense of fulfilment. You have now progressed through this book, creating clarity in your own purpose, understanding how to apply it to business in the world, starting the engagement of those around you and creating a culture that embraces and amplifies what you are about.

Consider, therefore, that this chapter is designed as a footnote of tips on leading such a purposeful life. The points below will help you consider how to maintain your momentum on the journey.

1. **Surround yourself with other purpose people.** Traditionally, friendships are based on proximity and we have a greater fondness for those with whom we spend more time. We build connections and friendships at various stages but, as you change and as you become more purposeful, some relationships fail to keep up and support our growth.

   When living purposefully, understand the need to evaluate relationships to ensure that they are mutually supportive. Don't drop your old school chum, but seek out and find other purpose-driven individuals. You will be able to help each other, possibly in business, but more so you will understand each other better and this can be helpful in a much softer manner.

Successful networks based on the like-minded, like The Knot in London or United Purpose in New York, demonstrate how these can flourish and support individuals in flourishing too.

Lord Janvrin says:

> *"Your values can be the same wherever you are. You may have to adjust the means but your basic values must be the same. There may be differences between what motivates people and those do change over time. But the point about values is that they're not fashionable. They're over and above that."*

2. **Take responsibility.** As a leader in business, you already know this, but particularly when you are leading purposefully, do not run away from your responsibilities, difficult conversations, challenges or problems. You do not blame others for what has gone wrong in your life.

You accept responsibilities for the results that you achieve. When you don't get the results you desire, you identify the changes that you can make and put a plan in place to make those changes.

Ben Fletcher says:

> *"On day one, it was easy for me as the managing director to stand up and say: 'Good news. Here's the purpose. This is the type of organisation we're going to be.' First, a lot of colleagues said that this was great. Then they said that if I really meant what I said, all these things needed to be sorted out. We had to turn around and tell them that a lot of things that were really familiar to them were not going to be on any more.*
>
> *"There's a period of transition and patience and perseverance that comes with that. You don't have an organisation that suddenly becomes different. You've got to work your way through it."*

3. **Be true, be authentic.** You have established absolute clarity in your mind as to who you are, your purpose, what your values are and what you want to achieve with your business and personally. You will dedicate your life in what is a noble endeavour and, as such, that gives you a strong moral compass, an authentic basis on which to make decisions and determine how you interact with others.

 Purpose, like integrity, is not something you leave at home or at the office. It pertains to everything you do and in that regard you will be seen as true, authentic and trustworthy with those who engage with you. But do make sure that your purposeful statements, plans and missions pass what journalists call the "sniff test".

Alex Mahon, CEO at The Foundry, a design, visual and 3D effects software firm, says:

> *"Any company can have a set of values, but do you actually wish them to be implemented through the organisation? Are they things you truly believe that the organisation truly stands for and do you push that through and gird yourself against it? Remember that Enron had a fabulous set of values but not everyone was following them."*

4. **Balance your efforts.** It doesn't matter if you use the Pareto principle that illustrates that 80% of your results will come from 20% of your efforts or simply determine your own way of prioritising. Whatever way you arrange your time, determine what you concentrate on.

Look at every area of your business, its clients, your time, your diary demands and ask yourself what are the areas you get most progress from? In theory, you could free up 80% of your time, concentrate on 20% of your work and still achieve 80% of your results. Focus on making significant things happen by refocusing on your priorities for purpose and performance.

5. **Set way markers.** Create some meaningful way markers on your purpose journey, both for the business and your personal state. If you focus on marching towards these within the business goals, but also perhaps with family, friends, further education and adventurous activities, you will find you not only make progress but that, when this is

achieved, you and others recognise it more so your achievements become a key part of your life story.

These way markers should be ambitious but achievable and linked directly to your purpose. When you achieve them, feel free to celebrate.

Paul Kahn at Airbus UK says:

> *"Our purpose has evolved by challenging our senior management on sustainability. We've signed up to the United Nations Global Compact. What does that mean in our factories and our business?*
>
> *"We actually need to be a force for good as well as a force to make things fly. I'd quite like that to go a stage further in terms of seeing it a bit more in people's faces in terms of how visible it is, but it's a journey. Five years ago, we wouldn't have had the level of visibility of priorities and engagement in the business that we have now."*

6. **Stop consuming for the sake of it.** On your purposeful path, consider making sensible choices on the spectrum between consuming ever more stuff and having more experiences. The latter creates a much greater sense of wellbeing and satisfaction than simply chasing the next version of a gadget.

Balance is key and purposeful people tend to understand when enough is enough, even if that varies from person to person.

As Tej Kohi says:

> *"There are only so many private jets and big cars and houses I can have. What would another billion mean to me?"*

7. **Create purpose time in your business day.** One problem that can arise is that normal running of the business can become overwhelming in terms of time and commitment. The phrase "I am too busy sawing to have time to sharpen the saw" applies to people who are so deeply immersed in their business that they don't have time to raise their heads to work on their business.

Create time in which you can lift yourself back up, remind yourself of the purpose and see how you stand at a more strategic level. Such thinking time can be invaluable for maintaining purpose power in both yourself and the business.

8. **Schedule something fun.** Every business will have a different view on what this might be. It may be doing sport, undertaking some great physical challenge and understanding something as simple as going to the theatre or having afternoon tea. Make some activities the things that you do as a team and make it a fun part of life. Doing meaningful charitable work together can also be fun.

Pat Gelsinger at VMware says:

> *"We now have 10,000 kids in the schools we helped to start in Kenya. I have recently visited some of our church's sponsorships in Ecuador and almost 100,000 kids in South America are part of the child sponsorship efforts we started.*
>
> *"Many of the VMware efforts are global in how we reach and serve our communities and send our people. We call it citizen philanthropy. Millennials and others coming into the workforce want to join companies that have higher purpose. They want to do things that make the world a better place.*

9. **Prioritise yourself.** This may sound contradictory and seemingly at odds if you have a particularly charitable purpose. But, if you want to be in the best position to help others and deliver your purpose, you must have around you everything you need to perform at your best.

If you end up living in a constant state of sacrifice where you always put the needs of others first, it will prove both unhealthy and unviable in the longer term. Don't deny others their place in your purposeful plan but invest in your own wellbeing and growth in order to continually develop for everyone's benefit. You will serve others much better that way.

Dame Inga Beale at Lloyd's of London says:

> *"You may also need to choose your battles. Sometimes you may need to decide not to fight that one today. It's not that important and you can put it on the back burner. There will come a time that you can do it."*

10. **Don't fear failure.** As a purpose-driven leader, you are always going to be exploring, trying new things and looking at innovative practices, products and services. You are, therefore, always taking a chance as you have chosen to become a risk-taker. Of course, you may well experience a little fear of failure at various stages, but when you are leading purposefully, you understand that, as long as you achieve a result, you can learn from it. If it is not the desired result, it can still be helpful and can inform the future.

Jon Bolton remembers the community impact of having to close a steel plant in Workington in Cumbria.

> *"It was a small plant but the impact of making a significant number of people redundant in a small town was huge. I still get emotional about it now. It is really, really difficult for all parties, not least of course for the employees and their families. You can't help but get involved personally and emotionally but it really was a question of doing something for the greater good.*

> *"Technically, we couldn't do what we wanted to do in Workington so the manufacturing of rail moved to Scunthorpe where we invested over £100m to build a world class facility that secured business and employment albeit in a different region. There was a whole load of pain and anguish but, had we not made that change then the business would have been lost completely and as well as losing the business in Workington, our Scunthorpe plant would itself have been far less secure."*

It is our strong hope that in reading this book you have been able to ask yourself questions about how purpose in yourself and in your business can drive performance and long-lasting sustainable success. We have detailed a path of key considerations which have helped many others and which can help you craft your own pathway.

Sometimes that pathway may appear lonely, but it isn't and others will converge and join with you at stages to help you on your journey. If you would like to share with us how you are doing, visit http://www.onehundredagency.com and let us know.

Finally – Keep being brave, something purpose is all about

CONTRIBUTORS

Dave Allen

Dave, founder of BrandPie, is a recognized expert in purpose-led transformation, brand strategy and brand architecture. His experience as a brand consultant has been built over 30 years. He first worked in consumer marketing for Kodak and then switched to consulting. He built and ran WPP's global brand consultancy The Brand Union with more than 750 employees in 23 countries. He also helped kick-start the WPP CSR program in 2002. His clients have included BP, Castrol, EY, General Motors, KPMG, L'Occitane, Mazda, RBC, Shell and Unilever. He established BrandPie in 2008 to get back to grass roots consulting. In 2009 he set up the BrandPie Foundation to help not-for-profits improve their marketing and brand building. The foundation's support has included creating the identity for Her Majesty the Queen's Diamond Jubilee volunteering initiative, The Jubilee Hour, which successfully mobilized 2.7 million volunteers and was recognized by the UK government as the largest mass mobilization since WW2. Other projects have included the UK's WW1 commemorative campaign "Remember WW1", the global re-branding of the international charity now known as "United Purpose" as well as Create, The Safe Water Network, The Liberty Science Center and The United Nations. He lives in New York. Dave believes business should be a force for good – creating wealth and employment and contributing to the stability of the communities they operate in.

Dame Inga Beale DBE

Dame Inga joined Lloyd's in January 2014. Previously she was group chief executive of Canopius, a prominent Lloyd's managing agent. Prior to that she spent four years with Zurich Insurance, including a period as global chief underwriting officer. She was group CEO of Converium, the Swiss mid-sized independent reinsurance company, leading a major turna-round of the business before it was acquired by SCOR in 2007. She started her career as an underwriter with Prudential before spending 14 years in international roles for GE Insurance Solutions. She is a member of the Government's Financial Services Trade and Investment Board and the Mayor's Business Advisory Board. In July 2016 she joined the board of the Chartered Insurance Institute.

Simon Belsham

Simon joined Notonthehighstreet.com in May 2015 as chief executive to build the brand's future growth and development as the leading curated online marketplace connecting the best small creative businesses with the world. Simon's career has been focused on unlocking the opportunities of technology and retail amidst evolving customer behaviours. Through his experience creating and growing online retail businesses at different points of inflection, Simon has gained invaluable insights to inform his vision for Notonthehighstreet.com and help support and grow the small creative businesses that define the brand.

Starting his career as a consultant at Cap Gemini in 2003, Simon joined Tesco and over seven years led a variety of projects developing the operat-ing model for the UK business, primarily in convenience, supply chain, general merchandise and latterly online with Tesco Direct.

In 2011, he joined Ocado as director of non-food, where he was respon-sible for building general merchandise platforms – the first of which was pet site fetch.co.uk – to link with Ocado's home delivery network. Simon re-joined Tesco in June 2013 as managing director of grocery home shop-ping and became online director, managing all online businesses, in January 2015.

Simon earned a BA in natural sciences and psychology at Cambridge University and an MBA from Harvard Business School.

Jon Bolton

Jon graduated from Newcastle Polytechnic in 1984 with a degree in elec-trical engineering and was sponsored by British Steel from the age of 17. After graduating, he held positions in operations for British Steel on Teesside, including a two-year spell as a shift engineer. Jon left Teesside to be chief engineer for the company's rail business based in Cumbria in

1989, and then moved to North Wales to be chief engineer for British Steel Coated Products for two years.

In 1995 Jon moved to the US and after a short spell in Cleveland Ohio, moved to Alabama where he was responsible for the construction and subsequent operations for a "mini mill" steel operation. In 2000 Jon returned to the UK as managing director of Corus Engineering Steels based in Rotherham and Sheffield. Two years later he was moved to France as MD of Corus Rail. During his four years in this job he moved the business to York.

In 2005 he was appointed as managing director of Teesside Cast Products and in 2010 he became director of long products business, assuming operational responsibility for businesses in Scunthorpe, Teesside, Rotherham, Glasgow and Hayange in France. In March 2016 Jon joined Liberty Group as CEO for its plates business and to head up its UK Steel Business Development activity. Jon is chairman of UK Steel and joint chair of The UK Steel Council with the Secretary of State. He is also a director of the Materials Processing Institute and chairman of the Prince of Wales's Industrial Cadet initiative which he started at the Prince's behest in Redcar. In 2016 he was appointed one of the Prince's national ambassadors for this initiative.

Edwin Booth

Edwin is executive chairman of E H Booth & Co, proprietors of Booths Food Stores in the north of England.

He represents the fifth generation of the family that has operated Booths since 1847. The procurement of wine became his speciality for many years, enabling Booths to gain national recognition for this important area of the business. Subsequently he developed a successful marketing function prior to becoming executive chairman in 1997. Edwin became an HRH The Prince of Wales Business Ambassador for the North West in 2005 and was finalist for the Ernst & Young – Master Entrepreneur of the Year (North) award. He has also been awarded the Institute of Directors Director of the Year for Lancashire and the North West and been recognised for his business pursuits by the North West Society of Chartered Accounts and as the Lancastrian of the Year in the Be Inspired Business Awards 2009. In 2010 Edwin was awarded an honorary doctorate by Lancaster University for his services to the region and his industry.

Edwin has worked with the Lancashire universities in the areas of leadership and business change programmes and chaired the Business in the Community advisory board for the North West from 2007 to 2014. He is vice-chairman of the Harris Charity which was co-founded by his forebear Edwin Henry Booth. Edwin is a founding trustee of the Prince's Countryside Fund and in June 2011 became chair of the Lancashire Local Enterprise Partnership.

Sir Richard Branson

Sir Richard is founder of the Virgin Group, which has expanded into many diverse sectors from travel to telecommunications, health to banking and music to leisure. Having started Virgin as a mail order record retailer in 1970, he founded Virgin Records. After the first Virgin artist, Mike Oldfield, released 'Tubular Bells', Virgin Records went on to sign household names from the Sex Pistols to The Rolling Stones. There are now more than 60 Virgin companies worldwide, employing approximately 71,000 people in over 35 countries.

Sir Richard has challenged himself with many record breaking adventures, including the fastest ever Atlantic Ocean crossing, a series of hot air balloon journeys and kite-surfing across the Channel. He has described Virgin Galactic, the world's first commercial spaceline, as being "the greatest adventure of all".

He is also a record-breaker online, voted the UK's number one Twitter user, the world's most social CEO and the world's most followed person on LinkedIn. He maintains a daily blog on virgin.com with more than 30 million followers across six social networks.

Since starting youth culture magazine *Student* aged 16, Sir Richard has found entrepreneurial ways to provoke positive change in the world. In 2004 he established non-profit foundation Virgin Unite to tackle tough social and environmental problems and strives to make business a force for good. Most of his time is now spent working with Virgin Unite and organisations it has incubated, such as The Elders, Carbon War Room, B Team, Oceans Unite and Branson Centre of Entrepreneurship.

Sir Richard was awarded a knighthood for services to entrepreneurship. He lives on Necker Island with his wife Joan, and has two children, Holly and Sam, and four grandchildren.

Carol Burke CBE

A career spanning more than 25 years and covering every level of the industrial landscape has helped position Carol as one of the UK's most forthright advocates of research and development and technology and skills, in particular developing the engineers of the future. As managing director of Unipart Manufacturing Group, she has overseen ten years of consistent growth and currently sits in charge of a profitable business turning over £151m and employing 800 people.

A graduate in mechanical engineering and management, she has been instrumental in changing the company's position to become a strategic partner to many of the world's original equipment manufacturers. This involves a three-tiered approach focusing on its own fuel rail products, bringing new technologies to market and transferring expertise into non-automotive sectors.

Carol, who worked for British Steel and GKN Axles in her earlier career, expects this strategy to generate £200m of sales by 2018.

She is also fiercely passionate about Unipart's involvement in the Institute for Advanced Manufacturing and Engineering, a £32m collaboration with Coventry University to create the UK's first "faculty on the factory floor".

Will Butler-Adams OBE

Will joined Brompton Bicycles in 2002, became director in 2006, and took over as managing director in 2008 and in this time grew the company from £2m turnover with 27 staff to £31m turnover with over 240 staff. He is a chartered engineer, passionate about all things engineering, having previously worked for DuPoint, Nissan and ICI. Will is married with three daughters and lives near Marlow. He is also chair of The Vibrant Economy Commission and trustee of the Education and Employer charity and Investors in People. He was a commissioner for the UKCES from 2013-16. Will is a fellow of the Royal Geographical Society, member of the Vintners company, a pilot and a keen vegetable gardener.

Dame Julia Cleverdon DCVO, CBE

Dame Julia is a passionate campaigner who has gained an international reputation for "connecting the unconnected", inspiring individuals and organisations to work together for the common good.

Having been chief executive of Business in the Community from 1991 to 2008 where she worked closely with the President HRH The Prince of Wales in building a movement of 850 member companies, she is now vice-president, working on encouraging responsible business practice in disadvantaged communities. Julia subsequently served as special adviser to The Prince's Charities, focusing particular effort on disadvantaged communities. Her objective, through all her work, is to build a more robust civil society by promoting collaboration among senior leaders from business, government, education and communities.

Julia has senior roles in charities transforming education and opportunities for young people. As chair and now vice-patron of Teach First, Julia pioneered efforts to address educational disadvantage by transforming exceptional graduates into inspirational teachers in low-income communities. Julia is also vice-chair of the Fair Education Alliance, an association of education and business organisations aiming to make education and life chances fair for all young people. She serves on the board of Teach for All, the international partnership with Teach for America to spread the mission to other interested social entrepreneurs across the world. Julia was appointed to chair the National Literacy Trust in 2013.

Following her 2012 government review on young people's engagement in social action Julia co-founded Step Up To Serve. Step Up To Serve, of which Julia is now a trustee, aims to get 60 % of young people involved in practical action in the service of others by 2020. Julia is also a board member of National Citizen Service, the Careers and Enterprise Company and the UK Holocaust Memorial Foundation.

Craig Donaldson

As chief executive of Metro Bank, Craig is responsible for providing executive leadership to the bank's rapidly expanding business. He is charged with guiding the bank's evolution from fresh, new entrant in retail banking to trusted financial services partner to millions of UK customers. From helping define Metro Bank's brand values, to hiring its inaugural employees and ensuring that the bank's staff deliver daily customer delight, Craig has been instrumental to Metro Bank from day one. Craig has prior experience in roles including managing director of retail products and direct channels at Royal Bank of Scotland, as well as senior roles with Barclays and HBOS. He has a degree in technology and management from the University of Bradford. Craig is a keen supporter of Sunderland AFC and has a young family.

Richard Ellis

Richard is vice-president, corporate social responsibility, at Walgreens Boots Alliance. He has spent the past 35 years working for companies on all aspects of the CSR agenda.

The early part of his career was spent in banking before becoming involved in CSR after the inner city riots of the early 1980s. After this involvement he held CSR related positions at HSBC, TSB and British Aerospace and ran his own CSR consultancy for five years.

In 2003 he joined Boots and became responsible for all of the company's CSR activities. Following the merger between Boots and Alliance UniChem and the subsequent private equity buyout, he was appointed director of CSR.

2014 saw the creation of Walgreens Boots Alliance following the merger between Walgreens in the USA and Alliance Boots. Richard now has responsibility for CSR globally for this new enterprise.

John Fallon

John became Pearson's chief executive on 1 January 2013. Since 2008 he had been responsible for the company's education businesses outside North America, and a member of the Pearson management committee. He joined Pearson in 1997 as director of communications and was appointed president of Pearson Inc. in 2000. In 2003, he was appointed CEO of Pearson's educational publishing businesses for Europe, Middle East & Africa. Prior to joining Pearson, John was director of corporate affairs at Powergen and was also a member of the company's executive committee. Earlier in his career, John held senior public policy and communications roles in UK local government. He is an advisory board member of the Global Business Coalition for Education and a member of the Council of the University of Hull.

Ben Fletcher

Ben was appointed managing director of Boots Opticians in October 2013 and was responsible for leading the business across 640 stores and 6,000 colleagues.

Boots Opticians was formed from the merger of Dollond & Aitchison and Boots Opticians in May 2009.

Ben was previously finance director of Boots UK & Ireland and joined Boots UK as commercial finance director in July 2011.

Prior to this, he was finance director for the global Salon Professional division at Procter and Gamble. During his 12 years there, Ben worked in a variety of finance roles in the UK and Western Europe.

Ben is a non-executive board member of the British Retail Consortium and chairs the Audit & Risk Committee. He is also a trustee of the National Literacy Trust. He left Boots Opticians in 2017.

Ryan Gellert

As general manager for Europe, the Middle East and Africa for active clothing brand Patagonia, Ryan oversees sales, marketing, sustainability and operational initiatives for the brand throughout the region.

Based at the European headquarters in Amsterdam, Ryan leads a team who live and breathe the Patagonia mission statement to build the best product, cause no unnecessary harm and use business to inspire and implement solutions to the environmental crisis.

An avid climber and backcountry snowboarder, Ryan has climbed and ridden throughout Asia, Europe, North America, Australia, the Middle East and South Africa. He has extensive experience of working with direct action environmental groups, serving on the boards of Access Fund and Protect Our Winters.

Prior to joining Patagonia, Ryan spent 15 years at Black Diamond Equipment, where he held a number of roles including brand president, vice-president of supply chain management and managing director of Black Diamond Asia.

Ryan holds a JD from the S J Quinney College of Law at the University of Utah; an MBA from Florida Institute of Technology and a BSBA in finance from the University of North Carolina, Charlotte.

Pat Gelsinger

Pat joined VMware in September 2012 and serves as the company's chief executive officer. Before VMware, he led EMC's information infrastructure products business as president and chief operating officer, overseeing engineering and operations for information storage, data computing, backup and recovery, security and enterprise solutions as well as the office of the chief technology officer. Prior to EMC, Gelsinger spent 30 years in numerous technical, management and executive roles at Intel, where he began his career. He led Intel's digital enterprise group, the company's largest business unit, and was responsible for enterprise products including the Xeon and Itanium processors. He also led the desktop products group, responsible for desktop processors, chipsets and motherboards for consumer and commercial customers.

Pat was Intel's first chief technology officer, and as the head of Intel Labs he led many of the company's research initiatives. He holds six patents in technology design, computer architecture and communications, is a well-known speaker on technology trends and has received a variety of industry awards.

Jay Coen Gilbert

Jay is co-founder of B Lab, a non-profit organization that serves a global movement of people using business as a force for good. Its vision is that companies compete not only to be the best in the world, but the best for the world and as a result society will enjoy a more shared and durable prosperity.

B Lab drives this change by building a global community of certified "B Corporations", promoting mission alignment using innovative corporate structures, to align the interests of business with society and help high-impact businesses be built to last. It helps tens of thousands of businesses and investors measure what matters and inspire millions to join the movement.

B Corporations meet rigorous standards of social and environmental performance and transparency, and expand their fiduciary duties to consider all stakeholders.

In 2016, there were over 1,700 Certified B Corporations in 50 countries.

Prior to B Lab, Jay co-founded and sold AND 1, a $250m basketball footwear and apparel company based outside Philadelphia.

Jay led AND 1's product and marketing and was AND 1's CEO during its period of most rapid growth and decline. Jay is a Henry Crown Fellow of the Aspen Institute, president of the board of the Philadelphia chapter of KIPP Philadelphia Schools, a growing cluster of high performing schools, and a former board member of Investors' Circle and Social Venture Network, leading national networks of social entrepreneurs and early stage social investors.

Jay grew up in New York City before attending Stanford University, graduating with a degree in East Asian studies in 1989. Prior to AND 1, Jay worked for McKinsey & Co and several organizations in New York's public and non-profit sectors. Between AND 1 and B Lab, Jay enjoyed a sabbatical in Australia and in Monteverde, Costa Rica, with his yogini wife Randi and their two children, Dex, 17, and Ria, 16. They live in Berwyn, Pennsylvania.

David Grayson CBE

David is professor of corporate responsibility at Cranfield School of Management. He joined the world of management education in 2007 after a 30-year career as a social entrepreneur and campaigner for responsible business and diversity.

This included founding Project North East (now PNE Group), an innovative economic development social enterprise which has worked in nearly 60 countries, and serving as a managing director of Business in the Community.

He has been a visiting senior fellow at the CSR Initiative of Harvard's Kennedy School of Government and a Visiting Fellow at several UK and American business schools.

David has chaired or served on charity, social enterprise and public sector boards, including the National Co-operative Development Agency, The Prince of Wales' Innovation Trust, the Strategic Rail Authority, Housing21 and the National Disability Council. He currently chairs Carers UK.

During his career, he has done work with numerous multinationals as well as for the OECD, EU and World Bank.

He sits on the corporate responsibility stakeholder advisory groups for Camelot and Lloyds Bank and is part of the circle of advisers for Business Fights Poverty and for the Asian Institute of Management's Ramon V. del Rosario, Sr. Center for Corporate Social Responsibility.

David is part of the faculty of The Forward Institute. He was awarded an OBE for services to industry in 1994 and a CBE for services to disability in

1999. He has written several books on responsible business, sustainability and social Intrapreneurism. His latest book is *Take Care: How to be a great employer for working carers.*

Stephen Greene

Stephen has a long and established career in volunteer engagement and pro-social marketing.

As chief executive and co-founder of RockCorps, he has delivered social engagement platforms in 10 countries, including 50 volunteer-exclusive concerts, featuring more than 100 music artists including Pharrell, Lady Gaga, Maroon 5 and Rihanna.

Stephen has created pro-social marketing partnerships with some of the biggest brands in the world, including Coca-Cola, Sprint, Orange/EE and Diageo.

His experience, combined with a deep understanding of and passion for social action and youth engagement, enables him to provide strategic counsel to a wide range of organisations across the public, not-for-profit and private sectors.

In November 2012, Stephen was appointed by the then Prime Minister, David Cameron, to be the founding chair of the NCS Trust, which is responsible for the management and delivery of National Citizen Service.

Stephen is also a trustee of: Good Gym, The Fowler Center and Young Camden Foundation, and serves as a judge for the Charity Governance Awards and Beacon Awards for Philanthropy. He earned an MBA from the Anderson School at UCLA. A proud native of Portland, Oregon, USA, Stephen currently lives in London.

Richard Harvey

Richard is a senior business leader and major philanthropist who amongst other senior roles served as group chief executive of Aviva from 2001 to 2007 and deputy chief executive from 2000 to 2001. He joined Norwich Union in 1992, holding senior positions in New Zealand and the UK, where he was deputy chief executive of CGNU and group chief executive, deputy chief executive and group finance director of Norwich Union.

He also chaired PZ Cussons and the Association of British Insurers and was a non-executive chairman of Jardine Lloyd Thompson. A fellow of the Institute of Actuaries, Richard holds a BSc Hons from University of Manchester.

Lord Robin Janvrin GCB GCVO QSO PC

Robin is a senior adviser to HSBC Private Bank (UK), an independent Crossbench member of the House of Lords, board member of the British Library and chairman of the Entente Cordiale Scholarship Scheme and the Prime Minister's Trade Envoy to Turkey. He is also a visiting fellow of the Oxford Centre for Corporate Reputation, Said Business School.

He served in the Royal Navy between 1964 and 1975 and subsequently joined the Diplomatic Service with postings abroad at NATO Brussels and New Delhi.

In 1987 he was seconded to Buckingham Palace as press secretary to The Queen, becoming assistant and then deputy private secretary to The Queen from 1990. In 1999 he took over as private secretary to The Queen, effectively her closest adviser and chief of staff with responsibilities for advising on all aspects of The Queen's public life. He stepped down in September 2007. Robin chaired the Royal Foundation of the Duke and Duchess of Cambridge and Prince Harry from 2010 to 2016, was a trustee of the National Portrait Gallery from 2008 to 2016 and sat on the board of the Gurkha Welfare Trust between 2010 and 2016.

Paul Kahn

Paul is president and chief executive of Airbus Group UK, responsible for the UK business, providing leadership, oversight and co-ordination of Airbus Group's activities and strategy in the UK. Paul is also responsible for the development of the group's strategic industrial partnerships within the UK, key customer relationships and for enhancing Airbus Group's relationship with the British Government.

In addition to his responsibilities at Airbus Group, Paul is a UK business ambassador for advanced manufacturing and aerospace, an ambassador for the Industrial Cadets and president of ADS, the UK's aerospace, defence, security and space trade body.

Paul joined Airbus Group from Thales in 2014, where he latterly held the position of president and chief executive of Thales Canada, leading a transformation in profitability, growth and customer relationships.

Prior to this, Paul spent over four years at Thales operations in Milan, Italy, as managing director of the navigation and airport solutions business line. With staff based across Europe and USA he led the development of disruptive surveillance technology and supplied ground infrastructure for navigation and airport systems worldwide. During this time Paul also held senior positions within the group's avionics division in the UK, and the strategy function, based in the Paris headquarters.

Paul began his career at the Ford Motor Company before joining the public sector as a civil servant at the UK Ministry of Defence. There, he led one of the major reviews of procurement processes. Paul has a Masters in engineering and management systems from Brunel University, London; he is a chartered engineer and a certified projects director. He holds an MBA from London Business School and attended the Royal College of Defence Studies.

An active outdoors person, he lives in Surrey and is married with three children. He holds dual British and American nationality.

Annabel Karmel MBE

With a career spanning 25 years, London born mother of three, Annabel Karmel, has pioneered the way families all over the world feed their babies and children.

Credited with starting a food revolution with her trusted recipes and methods, she has become the UK's leading children's cookery author, bestselling international author and the mother of all feeding experts with 43 cookbooks . . . and counting.

It all started with *The Complete Baby and Toddler Meal Planner* in 1991 – a book which has become the second best-selling non-fiction hardback of all time. It was a legacy to her first child Natasha who sadly died of a viral infection when she was just 3 months old.

Feeling vulnerable when her son Nicholas came along, she wanted to give him the very best foods. But she'd landed herself the world's fussiest eater. So she rolled up her sleeves and set to work on cooking up inventive combinations that Nicholas would love. Never in her wildest dreams did she think that these would culminate in a cookbook that would go on to sell over 4 million copies worldwide.

With the sole mission of raising the standards of children's diets, Annabel is a regular media commentator on food-related issues and she regularly undertakes consultancy work for major nursery chains, leisure resorts, restaurants and hotels worldwide.

Coupled with a vast digital following, recipe apps and cookbook-inspired supermarket food ranges, Annabel has become a leading pillar for parents who want to give their growing family the very best start in life.

In 2006, Annabel received an MBE in the Queen's Birthday Honours for her outstanding work in the field of child nutrition, and she has since become recognised as one of the UK's leading female entrepreneurs, becoming an inspirational role model for other rising stars, business start-ups, women in business and parents returning to work.

Graham Kerr

Graham has been chief executive of South32 since October 2014 and director since January 2015. Responsible for running all facets of the business, he successfully led the establishment of the company and its public listing in three countries in May 2015. Graham has a strong track record in global resource development and is passionate about health, safety and sustainability. Before joining South32, He worked in a wide range of roles across the BHP Billiton Group, including as chief financial officer from 2011 to 2014. He also spent two years at Iluka Resources as general manager, resources.

Graham has a business degree from Edith Cowan University and studied at Deakin University to become a certified practicing accountant.

Tej Kohli

Tej is chairman of Kohli Ventures, a venture capital company investing in entrepreneurs at the cutting edge of advances in technology. Kohli Ventures provides "smart capital" in the form of strategic advice and R&D, as well as financial investment, to companies harnessing the potential of technology for financial value and positive social impact. As founder of The Tej Kohli Foundation, Tej combines his philanthropic endeavours with his business experience to help the next generation of visionary entrepreneurs. The foundation supports projects tackling long-term social problems such as extreme poverty. One of the foundation's key areas of investment and research is the Tej Kohli Cornea Institute, which aims to end curable corneal blindness by 2030. Tej's career and experience stretch over 30 years and across the globe. After studying at the prestigious Indian Institute of Technology, he entered the tech world at a small tachometer manufacturer in Delhi and quickly spotted the potential of new technologies to transform and improve the industry. He founded the fintech firm Grafix Softech in the early 1990s and has established himself as a leader in the field of sustainable technology and corporate accountability. His expertise in business and technology and his knowledge of their potential to generate economic growth have been the dual driving forces behind his work. His interests in the fields of AI, robotics and life-extending genomics have led to his belief that emergent technologies have the power to transform and improve the lives of countless people across the globe.

Will King

Born in Lowestoft, Suffolk, in 1965, King of Shaves founder Will studied mechanical engineering at the University of Portsmouth and then worked in advertising sales and marketing in London. Following redundancy in the early 1990's recession, he created the King of Shaves brand as well as www. shave.com and the company's first product, a shaving oil sold at Harrods. King of Shaves is now celebrating its 24th anniversary, with more than seven billion lives saved? world-wide.

The company's innovations include issuing the King of Shaves shaving bond, the world's first mini bond, in June 2009.

Will has a particular interest in the financial technology sector and has coined the phrase "findustrial revolution"

He stood down as King of Shaves chief executive in October 2014 but remains the company's largest individual shareholder. He is currently involved in projects via his Entrepreneur-in-Residence Company and Savage & King, a creative agency for those who "Dare to Do", with his wife, creative director of Tiger Savage.

Will's favourite phrases are: "embrace change as a constant" and "enthuse, exceed, enjoy."

Jørgen Knudstorp

Jorgen is chief executive of the LEGO Group. His original ambition was to become a teacher, and he taught kindergarten for 18 months following his graduation (1987) from the Fredericia Gymnasium. He later attended Århus University, where he eventually earned masters and PhD degrees in economics and served as a lecturer. After a three-year stint with the management consulting firm McKinsey & Co, he was hired as LEGO director of strategic development. By 2003 he was the company's senior vice president of corporate affairs. When Jorgen was named CEO in September 2004, he became the first person from outside the family of LEGO Group founder Ole Kirk Christiansen to hold that position. Moving quickly to save a company that in 2003 had suffered losses of more than $300m, Jorgen implemented aggressive cost-cutting measures and shed underperforming businesses, most notably selling control of the company's four LEGOLAND theme parks for nearly $460m. He sharply reduced the development time for new products and in a highly popular move involved LEGO's many devoted adult fans in creative decisions through workshops in which new designs were discussed. LEGO's expansion into feature films also proved lucrative, with The LEGO Movie (2014) grossing some $470m worldwide. The movie's success helped LEGO surpass Mattel as the world's largest toy maker.

Hans Laessoe

As senior director, Hans headed strategic risk management within the LEGO Group, an area he established in 2006 and led for a decade. He has more than 35 years of experience at the group.

As strategic risk manager, he is responsible for leading the processes of managing strategic business risks, ensuring that risks and opportunities are identified holistically and addressed systematically, and deploying strategies.

Beyond this, as enterprise risk manager he is driving the liaison with operation, insurance, IT security, treasury and legal team ensuring reporting on the full LEGO Group enterprise risk portfolio.

The processes and approach developed and used by the LEGO Group have won multiple awards, and Hans has spoken at several conferences and written articles, books and other book materials. In April 2017, Hans established Aktus.dk, his own risk management consultancy.

Belsasar Lepe

A co-founder of Ooyala, Bel is senior vice-president of productions and solutions. In that role, he is responsible for product strategy as well as technology partnerships around the world, with a focus on building close and collaborative relationships with partners critical to the success of Ooyala clients.

Bel was born in Oxnard, California, the son of migrant farm workers, and spent his childhood following the growing seasons along America's west coast. Bel studied computer science at an early age, worked his way into Stanford University and eventually earned an engineering role at Google.

He and the two other Ooyala co-founders realized the major potential of delivering premium video content online and left the tech giant in 2007 to found Ooyala. They saw the need for technology that allowed major broadcasters, publishers and media companies to own their video experience, understand audiences via analytics and to deliver content to the host of devices available on the market.

Bel pushed the company into its global expansion throughout Latin America, Europe and Asia, specifically building its office in Guadalajara to encourage tech innovation in the region. He continues to drive innovation at Ooyala, integrating multiple video technology solutions to give customers more sophisticated solutions to solve today's increasingly complex challenges in video. Ooyala is building towards an integrated video platform, with the sole goal to drive down costs and maximize monetization for customers.

Alex Mahon

Alex is chief executive of The Foundry, a leading global developer of visual effects software for the design, visualisation and entertainment industries.

The company is headquartered in London, with offices in Silicon Valley, Manchester, Los Angeles, Shanghai, Dublin and Austin, and has a staff of 300.

Alex joined The Foundry to spearhead the next stage of its development following the company's acquisition by HgCapital for £200m in July 2015 and leads the team at a time of dynamic change and rapid growth. Prior to this, Alex was chief executive of Shine Group for three years, stepping down in July 2015 after successfully completing the sale of the company into a new joint venture between 21st Century Fox and Apollo Global Management. She joined Shine as managing director in 2006 and built the group through mergers, acquisitions and organic growth into an organisation with 27 creative labels in 12 countries and £700m in revenues alongside founder Elisabeth Murdoch. Ahead of this she had an extensive career in media organisations across Europe, at Talkback Thames, FremantleMedia Group and RTL Group.

Alex started her career as a PhD physicist and then worked at strategy consultants Mitchell Madison Group as an internet retail expert before leading the European Young Astronauts. She is a non-executive director of Ocado and The Edinburgh International Television Festival. Chairman of the RTS Awards, sh serves on the DCMS advisory panel on the BBC and is also Appeal Chair of The Scar Free Foundation, a national charity pioneering and transforming medical research into disfigurement. She lives in London with her four noisy children.

Timothy Melgund

Timothy is one of the longest-serving CEOs on the high street, having led Paperchase, the design led stationery and greeting cards retailer, for over 20 years.

After service in the Scots Guards, Timothy's early retail career was spent with WH Smith in a number of management roles across different businesses within the group. In the late 1980s, Timothy moved within WH Smith's Group to head up Paperchase, and in 1996 led a management buyout of Paperchase supported by private equity. Paperchase has changed hands twice since 1996; firstly to Borders Group, the now defunct US book retailing business and, in 2010, to private equity group Primary Capital. The management team has continued driving the business throughout.

Timothy actively pioneers product innovation, creativity and individuality within Paperchase, ensuring the brand is at the industry forefront and highly differentiated. His leadership has led a significant expansion of the Paperchase brand, both domestically and internationally. The Paperchase brand now has over 170 sites in the UK, an international concession business and rapidly growing proposition on line.

A qualified development surveyor, Timothy's expertise in property is evident in the Paperchase story. From the beginning of his time with the business, he has taken personal responsibility to establish an exceptional property portfolio and the company has a reputation for its discerning choice of property location.

Kieran Murphy

Kieran is president and chief executive of GE Healthcare Life Sciences, a $4bn molecular medicine business that provides industry-leading technologies and services for drug discovery, pre-clinical and clinical development and biopharmaceutical manufacturing, as well as molecular tools for therapy selection and treatment monitoring in patient care.

Kieran has more than 25 years' experience in the global life sciences and biotechnology industry, beginning his career with Janssen Pharmaceutical, a division of Johnson and Johnson, followed by leadership roles with Mallinckrodt, veterinary medicines provider Vericore, Novartis, Adprotech and Innovata. Prior to GE, Kieran was CEO of Whatman, a global supplier of filters and membranes for laboratory and medical diagnostic applications, which was acquired by GE in 2008.

Kieran earned his bachelor's degree in 1984 from University College, Dublin. He subsequently graduated from the University of Manchester Institute of Science and Technology with a master's degree in marketing.

Mike Perlis

Mike, chief executive of Forbes Media, is a media industry CEO with deep experience managing a wide range of content and multimedia brands. He joined Forbes in 2010 from SoftBank Capital, where he served as general partner for ten years and continues to be special partner. Before joining SoftBank, he served as president and chief executive of Ziff-Davis Publishing, publisher of *GQ*, president of Playboy Publishing, president of TVSM, publisher of *Runner's World* and *Men's Health*, chairman and CEO of IDG Peterborough and co-founder of New England Publications. He served on the board of Buzzfeed and was a board member and chairman of Associated Content. Previous board observer positions include GSI Commerce, *The Huffington Post* and KickApps. He is on the board of advisers of the Newhouse School of Public Communications at Syracuse University and is a trustee of Outward Bound International.

Paul Pester

Paul was appointed an executive director of TSB Bank on 31st January 2014. Having joined Lloyds Banking Group in 2010, he was appointed chief executive of the Verde programme in 2011 and led the development and establishment of the new TSB Bank within LBG. In 2013, Paul was appointed chief executive of TSB Bank and led the launch of the bank, its separation from LBG and its listings on the London Stock Exchange. In June 2015, TSB was acquired by Sabadell Group and Paul became a member of the group's global management committee. Previously, Paul spent six years as group chief executive of Virgin Money and two years working at Santander UK where he led the acquisition of Bradford & Bingley and the subsequent integration of Abbey, Alliance & Leicester and Bradford & Bingley to create a single UK business. His early career was spent in management consultancy, principally at McKinsey & Company.

Alison Platt CMG

Alison became chief executive of Countrywide in September 2014. Prior to her role at Countrywide, Alison was managing director at Bupa, responsible for international development markets. In addition to leading Bupa's businesses in India, Hong Kong, Thailand, Saudi Arabia, Poland and the US, Alison's role focused on driving growth in new markets for Bupa across South East Asia, China, the Middle East , as well as Europe and Africa. She took up this post in October 2012 having previously held a number of senior posts across Bupa including chief operating officer of its UK private hospitals business, deputy managing director in its UK insurance business and latterly managing director for its businesses in the UK, Europe and North America. Before joining Bupa Alison held a number of key positions in British Airways.

In April of 2016 Alison joined the board of Tesco as a non-executive director. Between 2012 and 2016 she was a non-executive director of Cable & Wireless Communications. From 2009 to 2013 she was chair of 'Opportunity Now', which seeks to accelerate change for women in the workplace. She was a non-executive director of the Foreign & Commonwealth Office between 2005 and 2010, and in the 2011 New Year Honours she was appointed a CMG for her services to the board of the Foreign and Commonwealth Office.

Paul Polman

Paul has been chief executive of Unilever since January 2009. Under his leadership, the group has set out an ambitious vision to decouple growth from its environmental footprint while increasing its positive social impact.

Paul is chairman of the World Business Council for Sustainable Development, a member of the International Business Council of the World Economic Forum and serves on the board of the UN Global Compact. He is also a member of the B-team and the European Resource Efficiency Platform.

Paul has been closely involved in global discussions on the Sustainable Development Goals and action to tackle climate change. In 2016, Paul was asked by the UN Secretary-General to be a member of the SDG Advocacy Group, tasked with promoting action on the 2030 Agenda. Prior to this, Paul served on the High Level Panel on the Post-2015 Development Agenda, presenting recommendations on the SDGs on behalf of the private sector.

He is also a member of the newly formed Business and Sustainable Development Commission, whose aim is to quantify the enormous rewards for companies that make the SDGs an integral part of the way they operate. In 2016, he received France's Chevalier de la Légion d'Honneur, in recognition of his efforts in galvanising sustainable business and for his involvement in the 2015 UN Climate Change Conference (COP21) in Paris.

Since 2010, Paul has been a non-executive director of the Dow Chemical Company.

In recognition of his contribution to responsible business, Paul has received numerous awards and accolades including WWF's Duke of Edinburgh Gold Conservation Medal (2013), the Centre for Global Development's Commitment to Development Ideas in Action Award (2013), the Rainforest Alliance Lifetime Achievement Award (2014), the UN Foundation's Champion for Global Change Award (2014), the Oslo Business for Peace Award (2015) and the UN Environment Programme's Champion of the Earth Award (2015).

Lord Mark Price CVO

Mark is a member of The House of Lords, a British businessman and the former managing director of Waitrose and Deputy Chairman of the John

Lewis Partnership. He worked at the JLP for 34 years. Mark was appointed Chairman of Business in the Community in January 2011, a post he held for four years, and was also appointed chairman of the Prince's Countryside Fund in 2010. He was awarded a peerage and joined the Conservative government as the Minister of State for International Trade in February 2016.

He was appointed a Commander of The Royal Victorian Order in the 2014 New Year's Honours.

Sir Michael Rake, FCA, FCGI

Sir Michael is chairman of BT Group and Worldpay Group. He is also a director of S&P Global and chairman of Majid Al Futtaim Holdings.

Mike's business roles also include chairman of the International Chamber of Commerce UK, his membership of the Advisory Council for Business for New Europe and board member of the TransAtlantic Business Council.

He is also a senior adviser for Chatham House and a member of the Oxford University Centre for Corporate Reputation Global Advisory Board. Mike is a William Pitt Fellow at Pembroke College, Cambridge. He is also vice-president of the RNIB. A former chairman of KPMG International, chairman of Business in the Community and easyJet and president of the Confederation of British Business, his non-executive roles have included non-executive director at Barclays, member of the Prime Minister's Business Advisory Group, chairman of Henley Festival and Trustee of the Prince of Wales Charitable Foundation.

Chuck Runyon

With more than 25 years of experience managing, owning and franchising health clubs, Chuck is an authority in the field of fitness. Chuck revolutionized the industry when he and Dave Mortensen co-founded Anytime Fitness – a no-frills alternative to "big-box gyms". Chuck and Dave designed smaller, neighbourhood clubs featuring the things members want most: convenience, affordability, quality equipment and surprisingly personable service in friendly, non-intimidating facilities. For his contributions to the fitness industry, in 2009, Chuck was honoured as the "John McCarthy Industry Visionary of the Year" by the International Health, Racquet, and Sportsclub Association (IHRSA). More recently, he was honoured by *Chief Executive* magazine with its inaugural "Leadership" award for his commitment to investing in people and relationships. Specifically noted were Chuck's efforts to help his employees become not merely more productive workers, but better people. Central to his leadership philosophy is the concept of "ROEI" – the return on emotional investment – which is characterized by an emphasis on people, profits, purpose and play.

Recognised as an expert on eliminating the barriers to healthy lifestyles, Chuck is frequently asked to speak or comment on issues related to why people claim that their health is a top priority now, while typically spending less than 1% of their time exercising.

Dame Stephanie Shirley DBE

Dame Stephanie is one of the UK's most successful IT entrepreneurs and an ardent philanthropist. Having arrived in Britain as an unaccompanied child refugee in 1939, she started what became Xansa (now part of the Sopra Group) on her dining room table with £6 in 1962. In 25 years as its chief executive she developed it into a leading business technology group, pioneering new work practices and changing the position of professional women (especially in high-tech) along the way. Her Damehood in the Millennium honours was for services to IT. She has served on corporate boards including Tandem Computers, the John Lewis Partnership and AEA Technology. Her philanthropy is based on her strong belief in giving back to society. She focuses on IT and autism (her autistic son Giles died aged 35 in 1998). Her charitable Shirley Foundation has made more than £67m of grants and initiated a number of projects that are pioneering by nature, strategic in impact and significant in money terms. Current activity is targeted at national strategies for autism.

Sir Tim Smit KBE

Sir Tim is executive vice-chairman and co-founder of the award-winning Eden Project in Cornwall. Eden began as a dream in 1995 and opened its doors to the public in 2000, since when more than 18 million people have come to see a sterile pit turned into a cradle of life containing world-class horticulture and startling architecture symbolic of human endeavour. Eden has contributed more than £1.7 billion to the Cornish economy. Sir Tim is a trustee, patron and board member of a number of statutory and voluntary bodies both locally and nationally. He has received a variety of national awards including The Royal Society of Arts

Albert Medal (2003). In 2002 he was awarded an Honorary CBE in the New Year's Honours List and In January 2011 he was appointed an honorary Knight Commander of the Most Excellent Order of the British Empire by Her Majesty the Queen in recognition of his services to public engagement with science. He has received Honorary Doctorates and Fellowships from a number of Universities. Sir Tim was voted "Great Briton of 2007" in the Environment category of the Morgan Stanley Great Britons Awards. In 2011 he was given a special award at the Ernst & Young Entrepreneur of the Year Awards, which recognises the contribution of people who inspire others with their vision, leadership and achievement. Sir Tim has taken part in a number of television and radio programmes and has been the subject of *This is Your Life* and a guest on *Desert Island Discs*. He is a regular speaker at conferences, dinners, awards ceremonies and other events. Sir Tim is also the author of books about both Heligan and Eden and has contributed to publications on a wide variety of subjects. He lives in Lostwithiel, Cornwall, and in his free time he enjoys reading, film, music and art.

Brad Smith

Brad Is chairman and chief executive officer of Intuit. He joined Intuit in 2003 and held a series of executive positions during a five-year rise through the company where he successfully led several of its major businesses. He was named Intuit's president and chief executive officer in January 2008 and became chairman of the board of directors in January 2016.

Building on Intuit's strong foundation and enduring mission, Smith has cultivated an agile, innovative culture and led initiatives to reimagine and reinvent Intuit to harness emerging technology and trends, continuing to improve the financial lives of customers around the world. During that time, Intuit has earned a reputation as an innovative company that is consistently ranked as one of the top 100 best places to work, and among the most-admired software companies each year.

Before being named CEO, Smith was senior vice-president and general manager of Intuit's Small Business Division, which included the portfolio of QuickBooks, Quicken and Payroll products. Previously he led the company's Consumer Tax Group, which produces TurboTax, the nation's leading consumer tax preparation software. He began his Intuit career leading the Accountant Central community, cultivating relationships and delivering services for accounting professionals.

Smith earned his master's degree in management from Aquinas College in Michigan and a bachelor's degree in business administration from Marshall University in West Virginia.

Cilla Snowball CBE

Cilla joined AMV BBDO in 1992 as the agency's first new business director. Twenty-five years later, she is now chairman and group chief executive, overseeing the three companies that comprise the AMV Group in the UK – AMV BBDO, Proximity and Redwood.

Cilla sits on the boards of BBDO Worldwide and Derwent London plc and she chairs the Women's Business Council. She was awarded the CBE in the 2009 New Year's Honours list for services to the advertising industry.

Most importantly, she is Fred, Albert and Rosie's mum.

Alli Subaskaran

Subaskaran is the entrepreneurial founder and chairman of Lyca Group.

Born in Mulllaitivu, Sri Lanka, to a working-class family, he lost his father at a young age and was brought up by a single working mother. During the country's civil war, his family migrated to Paris in 1989, beginning a business selling calling cards for people to make overseas phone calls. This developed into a production and distribution company that led to the family moving to London in 1999. In 2002, Subaskaran founded Lycatel, an international calling card company, with the vision of growing the brand into a global leader. Lycamobile was launched in 2006, spearheading growth to 21 markets across five continents, with the original Lycatel team growing from 10 employees to 1,500 by 2006, and more than 8,000 today.

Lycamobile is now the world's largest international mobile virtual network operator and market leader in international prepaid mobile calls, with more than 15 million customers across 21 countries.

Lyca Group meanwhile is the world's largest provider of products and services to ethnic and international communities, delivering products and services across the technology, media and telecoms, financial services, transport, healthcare and entertainment sectors. It plans to grow to more than 50 million customers by 2020 and launch in at least 20 new countries within four years. In 2010 Subaskaran founded Lyca's Gnanam Foundation with his mother, Gnanambikai Allirajah, and wife, Prema, to support displaced and vulnerable individuals and communities impacted by conflict and climate change. Aiming to empower displaced communities to build self-sufficient and sustainable livelihoods through a focus on healthcare, education, training and housing, it has worked with charities including the British Asian Trust, Save the Children and Muslim Aid.

Sally Tennant

Sally acts as an Independent Wealth Management Adviser. She is chairman of Duncan Lawrie Private Banking, chair of Style Research, the portfolio analytics company, a director of Fiorucci and Ledunfly and vice-chairman of the Advisory Board of Paladin Capital Group. From 2011 to 2014 Sally was chief executive of Kleinwort Benson. She was previously chief executive of Lombard Odier (UK) Ltd and chief executive of Schroders Private Banking. Her earlier career was in asset management at Gartmore, Morgan Grenfell Asset Management and SG Warburg. Sally is a patron of Tommy's the Baby Charity, a trustee of the STARS Foundation, and a trustee of Guy's & St Thomas's Charity, where she sits on the investment and audit committees. She holds a degree in politics from the University of Durham.

Iqbal Wahhab OBE

Iqbal has lived in Britain for almost his whole life and in a career spanning 30 years he has built a reputation for delivering world-class excellence through his highly successful restaurant businesses, Roast and The Cinnamon Club. It was Iqbal's early experience in the media which saw him run his own hospitality PR business and Indian food publication, *Tandoori Magazine*, that launched his career in the restaurant industry. In 1999, Iqbal sold out *Tandoori Magazine* and created the multi-award winning Cinnamon Club in 2001 – a restaurant and bar aimed to change the way we view Indian dining. In 2003 he co-authored *The Cinnamon Club Cookbook* and in 2005 opened the Roast, the British restaurant and bar in London's Borough Market. Iqbal has won a number of major awards and accolades during his career. He was voted one of the top ten restaurateurs in Britain in an *Independent on Sunday* survey and listed in the Caterer

Power 100, GQ 100 Most Connected and *The Sunday Times* Maserati Top 100 business start-up mentors. He has received an honorary doctorate in Business Administration from the University of East London and an honorary doctorate in science from the University of West London. He chairs two social enterprises – Mum's The Chef and Bounce Back and is actively engaged in the prison reform agenda. In 2016 he wrote *Charity Sucks*, a polemic published by Biteback.

Robin Wight CVO

Robin is the founder of the Ideas Foundation and president of Engine Group and has been working in the advertising industry for almost 50 years. He began his career by setting up a student advertising agency while he was still an undergraduate at Cambridge. After working as a copywriter in a number of agencies, including Collett Dickinson Pearce and Partners, he co-founded Wight Collins Rutherford Scott (WCRS) with Peter Scott in 1979. WCRS grew to become one of the most influential agencies in the UK advertising industry, with Robin helping to create iconic campaigns for brands like Carling Black Label, Orange and BMW. In 2004, Robin was part of the management team that led the management buyout of Havas, creating Engine. Though Robin has spent his whole career in advertising, he has also been highly involved in a number of outside interests. From 1992 to 2002, he was chairman of the Duke of Edinburgh's Award, Charter for Business, which has since raised over £40m. From 1997 to 2005 he was chairman of Arts and Business which encourages British businesses to invest £140m a year in support for the arts. In the 2000 Birthday Honours Robin was awarded a CVO for his services to the Duke of Edinburgh's Award, Charter for Business.

In 2003 he founded the Ideas Foundation, a charity which helps identify and nurture creatively gifted young people from ethnic minorities through the award of Creativity Scholarships.

Thanks also to inspiration provided by

John Adair

John had a colourful early career, serving as a platoon commander in the Scots Guards in Egypt and then becoming the only national serviceman to serve in the Arab Legion, where he became adjutant of a Bedouin regiment. After national service, he qualified as a deckhand in Hull and worked on an arctic trawler in Iceland waters. He then worked as a hospital orderly in the operating theatre of a hospital.

After being senior lecturer in military history and adviser in leadership training at the Royal Military Academy Sandhurst, and associate director of The Industrial Society, in 1979 John became the world's first professor of Leadership Studies at the University of Surrey.

Between 1981 and 1986 John worked with Sir John Harvey-Jones at ICI introducing a leadership development strategy that helped to change the loss-making, bureaucratic giant into the first British company to make a billion pounds profit.

John has written over 40 books, translated into many languages. Recent titles include *How to Grow Leaders* and *Effective Leadership Development*. He is also a teacher and consultant.

Charles Handy CBE

Charles is an Irish author/philosopher specialising in organisational behaviour and management. Among the ideas he has advanced are the "portfolio worker" and the "Shamrock Organization" (in which professional core workers, freelance workers and part-time/temporary routine workers each form one leaf of the "Shamrock"). Handy's business career started in marketing at Shell International.

He left Shell to teach at the London Business School in 1972 and spent a year in Boston observing the Massachusetts Institute of Technology's way of teaching business. He was chairman of the Royal Society of Arts from 1987 to 1989. He has honorary doctorates from Bristol Polytechnic (now the University of the West of England), UEA, Essex, Durham, Queen's University Belfast and the University of Dublin. He is an Honorary Fellow of St Mary's College, Twickenham, the Education City and Oriel College, Oxford. He was awarded a CBE in 2000.

Peter Drucker

Peter was one of the world's most distinguished business theorists, starting as a teacher, then professor of politics and philosophy at Bennington College from 1942 to 1949. He then spent 22 years at New York University as a professor of Management from 1950 to 1976. Peter went to California in 1971, where he developed one of the country's first executive MBA programs for working professionals at Claremont Graduate University, then known as Claremont Graduate School. From 1971 until his death, he was the Clarke Professor of Social Science and Management at Claremont. Claremont Graduate University's management school was named the Peter F. Drucker Graduate School of Management in his honour in 1987. He established the Drucker Archives at Claremont Graduate University in 1999; the archives became the Drucker Institute in 2006. He continued to act as a consultant to businesses and non-profit organizations well into his nineties. He died in 2005.

Dame Anita Roddick DBE

Dame Anita 23 October 1942 – 10 September 2007) was a trend-setting ethical businesswoman, human rights activist and environmental campaigner. She is best known as the founder of The Body Shop, an international cosmetics company producing and retailing natural beauty products that helped shape the ethical consumerism. The company was one of the first to prohibit the use of ingredients tested on animals and one of the first to promote fair trade with third world countries.

Dame Anita was involved in activism and campaigning for environmental and social issues, including involvement with Greenpeace and The Big Issue. In 1990, she founded Children on the Edge, a charitable organisation which helps disadvantaged children in eastern Europe and Asia. She believed that business should offer a form of moral leadership, as that is a more powerful force in society than religion or government. Dame Anita died in September 2007.

As part of the supportive research for this book, Bean Research Ltd were commissioned to conduct research among 100 corporates, entrepreneurs, social enterprises, purpose leaders and commentators on behalf of One Hundred Partners. This complemented the 50 in-depth face-to-face interviews with a variety of senior business leaders. We are extremely grateful to the following who were willing to be named as having contributed their views as well as those who chose to remain anonymous:

A.M. "Bobby" Brumfield, Leonum Advisors

Alan Coates, Knowledge Peers

Alex Mackenzie, OneLeap

Amanda Lyons, Gong Communications

Anne Heal, Volunteering Matters

Arabella Simpkin, Greyscale Spaces Limited

Ashley Bivens, Taylor Wessing

Ashley Lawrence, Ex-military Careers Ltd

Ashley Sweetland, CBRE

Chris McManus, LOccitane

Cliff Prior, Big Society Capital

David Wilson, Engage Works Ltd

Donald Fogarty, FutureRising Ltd

Dr. Colleen Becker, Sampson Solutions Ltd

Edwina Hughes, Sodexo

Eldad Umenjoh, Ajong Young Farmers, Cameroon

Elin Haf Davies, aparito Ltd

Emma Price Thomas, ArcelorMittal

Gintare Matuzaite, Amberoot

Gordon Mizner, Engineering Development Trust

Greg Chant-Hall, Skanska/ Square Gain

Helen Stucky Weaver, Wellness Weavers

Ian Blythe, Walgreens Boots Alliance

Ilaria ida Walton, Unilever

Jack Graham, Year Here

James Perry, LocoSoco

Jamie Gray, Buddy Burst

Jamie Lyons, Bell Pottinger

Jane Langley, Bluepatch

Jemma Macfadyen, Spinnaker Consulting

Jeni Becker, Junior Achievement of Greater SC

Jennifer Tankard, Responsible Finance

Jenny Dawson Costa, Rubies in the Rubble

John Canady, National Philanthropic Trust UK

Jon A. Weiss, EQi group

Jonathan May, Hubbub

Judith Houston, LEGO

Julie Lyle, USA Global Retail Marketing Association

Karl Rego, London Executive Advisors Ltd

Les Ratcliffe, Jaguar Land Rover

Marcus Morrell, Arup

Marg Mayne, Mytime Active

Michael Alexander, Diageo

Michelle Bennett, University of Delaware

Nadine Exter, Cognisus
Nathalie Clément, KPMG
Navid Akhtar, Alchemiya Media
  Limited
Nurzulfikar Ali Bin Gulam Kasmi,
  Prudential
Oonagh Harpur, The Crowd, WBA
  and GLD
Patrick Harrison, Weber
  Shandwick
Peter Conlon, Ammado AG
Peter Gassiraro, Durable Digital
Peter Hughes, Pearson
Philip Taylor, global marketing
  professional
Rachel Jones, Fit N Fun Kids,
  Enterprise Foundation
Ravinol Chambers, Be Inspired
  Films
Richard Brophy
Richard Cobbett, Social Enterprise
  Mark CIC
Richard Leftley, MicroEnsure
Richard Spencer, BT
Rob Compton, Cass Business
  School

Robin Boles, LVO, In Kind Direct
Russell Dalgleish, Exolta Capital
  Partners
Saba Shaukat, ECO Capacity
  Exchange
Sally Sykes, BMI Healthcare
Sara Baptiste-Brown, Pivot
Sara Williams, Staffordshire
  Chamber Commerce
Sophie Hackford, Sophie Hackford
  Ltd
Stafford Lloyd, Riversimple
Stephen Greene, RockCorps
Stephen Pegge, Lloyds Banking
  Group
Steven Henry, Chalmor Ld
Tamina Mir, Women Buzz
Tauna Dean, adidas Group
Tiffany Arntson, Rogue Matters
Tom Manimanakis, Ethos Assets
Trevor Hutchings, WWF UK
Uzair Bawany, Fairway Search
  Partners
Yasmin Waljee, Hogan Lovells
Zoe Le Grand, Forum for the
  Future

INDEX